Important Inform
About this Print on Den

D1706791

The materials described in this book were redesigned in 1998 to meet the needs of today's choir leaders. The new materials are called *Children's Music Series®*. The following list describes which *Children's Music Series®* products are comparable to products described in this book.

The Music Leader–combination of the following:
• *Plans & Pluses*
• a Pak (*Music & Me Pak*–age 3 or *Music Time Pak*–ages 4-K)
• *Songs for Music Time Songbook* (for ages 4-K)

Music for Threes–*Music & Me Pak*
Preschool Resource Kit–*Music Time Pak*

Music for Threes Cassette–*Music & Me Cassette* or *CD*

Preschool Music Cassette–combination of the following:
• *Songs for Music Time Cassette* or *CD* (annual products; not included in Pak)
• *Music Time Activity Cassette* or *CD* (quarterly products; included in Pak)

Music Time–still available

To order *Children's Music Series®* materials:
• Phone (1-800-436-3869)
• Write LifeWay Church Resources Customer Service, 127 Ninth Avenue, North, Nashville, TN 37234-0113
• FAX (615) 251-3810
• EMAIL CustomerService@lifeway.com

If you have questions about your choir or *Children's Music Series®*, EMAIL PreschoolMusic@lifeway.com.

How to Lead Preschoolers in Musical Activities

RHONDA J. EDGE AND BARBARA SANDERS

CONVENTION PRESS / NASHVILLE, TENNESSEE

Acknowledgments

The authors of *How to Lead Preschoolers in Musical Activities* owe a debt of gratitude to the authors, editors, and shapers of *Guiding Fours and Fives in Musical Experiences* and *Leading Preschool Choirs*. Until recent years, musical experiences for preschoolers meant musical experiences for only fours and fives. With the release of *Music for Threes* in 1988 and *Musical Experiences for Preschoolers; Birth Through Three* in 1989, musical experiences for preschoolers took on new meaning. Now, music for preschoolers means music for the unborn child, babies, ones, twos, threes, fours, and fives.

Special thanks is due Dr. Betty Bedsole, associate professor of church music, The Southern Baptist Theological Seminary, Louisville, Kentucky, and G. Ronald Jackson, preschool/younger children's consultant of the Church Music Department, the Sunday School Board of the Southern Baptist Convention for evaluating the manuscript.

Gratitude is also expressed to the early dreamers who had the responsibility of determining the content and scope of this book and *How to Lead Children's Choirs*. The team consisted of the four writers—Mary DeLaine Allcock, Madeline Bridges, Rhonda Edge, Barbara Sanders—and the design editors Sheryl Davis Tallant, Clinton E. Flowers, and Derrell Billingsley. This team did its work under the guidance of Bill F. Leach, Senior Manager, Preschool/Children's Materials Development Section, Church Music Department, The Sunday School Board of the Southern Baptist Convention.

Contents

Introduction

How to Lead Preschoolers in Musical Activities is an ambitious title. It indicates what you can expect to learn from this book, which is designed for leaders of preschoolers in all church program organizations—Sunday School, Discipleship Training, and Church Music. While this book is written for preschool leaders in church, parents can use a large majority of the suggestions and activities with their preschoolers at home. Parents will find it to be a valuable guide in providing a beneficial musical environment for their preschoolers.

This book discusses planning and conducting musical activities for the following age groups: birth through twos, threes, and fours and fives. It also addresses how each age group responds to music and what you may expect when leading musical activities for them. Understanding the developmental stages of preschoolers, which is vital to planning and conducting effective musical activities, is covered in Section 1.

The material in these pages is based on the same basic principles of music education that have served Southern Baptists so well for many years, but you will also find new ideas, activities, and updated methods for leading preschoolers in musical activities.

Preschoolers learn through *doing.* They acquire concepts or understandings as a result of their experiences. Learning takes place as they gain greater understanding of knowledge they already have stored in their minds. Developing spiritual and musical understandings through musical activities helps preschoolers develop skills in listening, singing, moving, and playing instruments.

The charts in the back of this book, and those in *How to Lead Children's Choirs,* * give an overview of the approach used in guiding the musical learning of preschoolers and children. By placing the two charts side-by-side you will see the total scope and sequence of the preschool and children's choir curricula presented in the two books and in the basic curriculum materials: *The Music Leader,* ** *Music Time,* ** *Music*

Makers, * * *Young Musicians,* * * and *The Children's Choir.* * *

Preschoolers in today's Southern Baptist churches benefit from 50 wonderful years of unparalleled growth and development in church music. The Church Music Department of the Baptist Sunday School Board was established in 1941, setting the stage for the development of a program that is unmatched by any other denomination in America. When the first article about using music with preschoolers at church appeared in *The Church Musician,* some of the methodologies now exerting the greatest influence on music education were just being introduced in this country. Because Southern Baptists have always incorporated the best in curriculum planning, the methodologies and teaching techniques of Carl Orff, Zoltan Kodály, Emile Jaques-Dalcroze, and many others have been researched, tested, and used when those techniques proved to be effective.

Music is a powerful tool, so let us use it effectively. Musical activities with preschoolers not only will help shape their lives but also may influence the future of music in the Southern Baptist Convention far into the next century. The opportunity for preschool leaders is compelling; the responsibility is awesome.

This book is organized into six sections. Section 1 deals with understanding preschoolers; Section 2 with laying spiritual, musical, and church music foundations; and Section 3 with organizing and planning for preschoolers. Section 4 concerns music for babies birth through two; Section 5, music for threes; and Section 6, music for fours and fives. A glossary of terms, the Preschool Development Chart, Personal Learning Activities, and The Study Course complete the book. May *How to Lead Preschoolers in Musical Activities* help you become a more effective leader.

---

*Available at Baptist Book Stores or by calling toll free 1-800-458-BSSB.

**Available from the Customer Service Center, 127 Ninth Avenue, North, Nashville, Tennessee 37234, or by calling toll free 1-800-458-BSSB.

1

Understanding Preschoolers

Development of the Unborn Child

Physical Development—Physical changes occur rapidly in the unborn child. The brain and head area and the circulatory system are the first areas to develop between the second and eighth weeks after conception. During the third month of life, the child begins responding physically due to the development of the nervous system. By the fourth month of life, he can move quickly and make reflex actions. By the seventh month of life, he can inhale, exhale, and cry.

Mental and Emotional Development—No one really knows everything about a child's mental and emotional development in the womb, but it is known that the child responds by moving when he hears loud noises or when the mother listens to certain types of loud music. Some mothers even report their child kicks rhythmically when hearing music with a quick, steady beat, such as music from the Baroque period. Encourage parents to listen to music and sing for the child, giving him different types of aural experiences.

Spiritual Development—The unborn baby will benefit from hearing his parents and siblings sing and speak. Parents should be encouraged to prepare for the baby's arrival by singing songs that will be sung to the child after he is born. Siblings also will benefit from learning and singing songs to the unborn baby. Parents should include hymns and hymn fragments in family devotions.

Development of Babies

Physical Development—Between birth and three months of age, babies change rapidly even though they spend half of their time asleep. They are born with several reflex actions, but, by the second month after birth, they begin functioning mentally and emotionally. They coordinate their movements to the sound of human voices they hear.

During the third month, babies can hold their heads steady and begin to reach for objects above their heads. They sit up with adult support by four months and can roll over by five months. By six months, they are very active and repeat actions. They follow objects with their eyes and will grab objects while sitting on an adult's lap.

From six to nine months, babies continue to change rapidly. At six months, they have doubled their birth weight. They teethe, chew, bite, and grow quickly. Their hearing skills are developing, and they respond to their names. Their eye-hand coordination also is developing, and they like to grab red and yellow objects. By seven months, babies are almost ready to creep and crawl because they roll over on their stomachs and are beginning to develop depth perception. They like to examine objects. They recognize their mothers' faces. At eight months, they can sit without an adult holding them and can pull up and stand. They like to ring bells and move noisemakers.

From nine to twelve months, babies' gross motor skills are fairly well-developed. At nine months, they can use their fingers when eating, hold and drink from a cup, pull up and sit, creep and crawl, and cruise around the playpen. By ten months, they can stand by pulling up to furniture, and they like to shake bells and rattles. They creep and stand alone at eleven months and begin speaking a few words.

Mental and Emotional Development—From birth, babies use their senses to learn. They like human sounds more than nonhuman sounds. They communicate their needs by crying. By the second month, they make eye contact with their care givers.

From three to six months, babies coo, smile, and babble. They need parents and other care givers to respond to their sounds. They like the sounds of rattles and other shaking toys. They only realize that their care givers exist when they see them. By the fourth or fifth month, they begin to understand the cause and effect of their own actions. They begin to feel and express emotions of joy, contentment, fear, and anger. They look with interest at a person who is speaking or singing. By the fifth or sixth month, they become very aware of their environment and want to touch and look at objects. They need adults to provide physical needs, comfort, cuddling, eye contact, and attention.

At six months, babies are beginning to recognize their parents and are afraid of strangers. They show likes and dislikes. They babble and try to imitate adults. They also look at the direction from which sounds come. At seven months, they like to play peekaboo and love to respond to their names. By eight months, they label familiar objects, such as family pets, by making the sound of the object. They cry and yell loudly to get adults to look at them.

By nine months, babies try to please their mothers and imitate vocal inflections they hear. They try to be independent at ten months. They like to look at pictures in books, see finger plays, try to make sounds, and play nursery games. They understand simple commands. At eleven months, babies like to creep, chase, and throw objects. They like to help when they are being dressed and try to make speech sounds.

Moral and Spiritual Development—A proper foundation for babies' moral and spirital development is laid when love is shown to them and Christian values are practiced in the home. Songs with biblical texts should be sung, and simple Bible thoughts and church-related picture books should be read to babies. Most importantly, parents and other care givers should show them love and acceptance at every opportunity.

Development of Ones

Physical Development—One-year-olds must be watched constantly by parents and care givers. From 12 to 18 months, they are in constant motion, cruising around the room, grasping objects, walking, climbing, and not realizing their activities may be dangerous. They like to place objects in and remove them from a cup or bottle. They like to carry objects and pull toys. They are able to play with cubes, books with cardboard pages, large crayons and paper, form boards, and large plastic beads.

From 18 to 24 months, ones learn how to run. They love to climb stairs and other objects and throw balls. They like to empty trash cans and other containers and enjoy drawing on paper and building with blocks. They are also beginning to toilet train. By 19 months, they can eat with a spoon. By 20 months, they can kick a ball, stack blocks, and push and pull toys. By 22 months, they can ride a tricycle and assemble toys with simple parts. By 23 months, they jump, climb, and like to run more than they like to walk. At 24 months, they are able to undress themselves.

Mental and Emotional Development—Ones grow rapidly mentally and emotionally from 12 to 18 months. They can speak a few words that are usually tied to a motor action, such as *hello* and *bye*. At 13 months, they like to look at pictures in books and play with toys. They feel jealous, affectionate, angry, and afraid. Ones react to situations the way their parents do. By 14 months, they repeat words they do not understand. They are afraid of the dark. Around the age of 15 months, they can speak two- and three-word sentences and know the names of people important to them. They like being helpers.

By 16 months, ones like to watch children's television shows and like for adults to invent stories about pictures in their books. Seventeen-month-olds like to imitate and echo adults. They like to bathe and want to feed and dress themselves.

At 18 months, ones have a vocabulary of about 10 words. They throw temper tantrums because they cannot clearly express themselves verbally. They know which objects are theirs. At 19 months, they like name-labeling games. They can point to objects and body parts. They enjoy imaginary conversations on toy telephones. By 20 months, ones try to speak sentences. They like nursery rhymes, and they can recognize themselves in the mirror. Twenty-one-month-olds like two-piece puzzles and form boards, and they like to look at pictures of familiar persons. By 22 months, they can name food items at the table. By 24 months, they will tell care givers when they need to eat, drink, or use the toilet.

Moral and Spiritual Development—Parents should emphasize to one-year-olds that God loves them, Jesus loves them, and Jesus is their friend. God and Jesus should be talked about as important members of the family. Parents should sing Bible songs and read books in the Bible-and-Me Series* to their children. They should make music a part of family devotion times and take their children to church. Above all, they should remember that children develop morally and spiritually through adult example.

Development of Twos

Physical Development—From 25 to 30 months, twos grow rapidly. They like to walk, jump, tumble, run, climb, and pick up and throw objects. Because they are growing quickly, they are accident prone. They like to build block towers, work puzzles, string beads, unscrew jar lids, and play with modeling clay.

From 31 to 36 months, twos walk and run well. They can walk up and down stairs without adult assistance. They can jump with both feet and hop on one foot. Their brains are growing quickly, and their motor skills are improving.

Mental and Emotional Development—Twenty-five- to 30-month-olds want to please adults but are afraid of strangers. They are self-centered and like to play alone instead of in groups. They are becoming independent from their mothers. They like to imitate adults. They are ritualistic and complain if they cannot keep the same routine. Twos are afraid of objects such as vacuum cleaners and drains. Both boys and girls like to play with dolls. They like books and songs with repetitive texts. They like to play with dolls, modeling clay, and three-piece puzzles. They like to play in sandboxes and on slides and jungle gyms.

From 31 to 36 months, twos become selfish and disobedient, talk constantly, and like to say no. They are extremely ritualistic and want to be independent. They still do not understand the concept of sharing and need adult assistance in group activities. They like dramatic play and enjoy playing on the floor. They like playing with modeling clay, stringing beads, painting, playing with block trains, and putting shapes in form boards. They like to have stories read to them and like to name objects they see pictured in the books.

Moral and Spiritual Development—Thirty-one- to 36-month-olds are able to communicate verbally with care givers. They need to learn the difference between right and wrong and that some actions are improper. At the same time, they need to feel love and Christian values from adults. Because their concepts of God and Jesus result from what they think about adults, adults should respond calmly to them. They learn about God through their everyday activities and through music. They learn about Jesus through their parents and others. They can pray at meals and sing thanks to God. They like to go to church and to be involved in family devotion times.

Development of Threes

Physical Development—Three-year-olds have better developed large muscle skills than small muscle skills. From 37 to 42 months, they can run easily, stand on one foot, climb a jungle gym, catch and throw a ball, and walk a straight line. They can dress themselves, brush their teeth, wash and dry their hands, and build with blocks.

From 43 to 48 months, their large muscle development allows them to tiptoe, hop, jump, and walk and run smoothly. Girls are usually more physically developed than boys. Threes' small muscle activities include cutting with scissors and building block towers.

Mental and Emotional Development—From 37 to 42 months, children tend to be agreeable most of the time. They like to talk and want to hear adults read so they can hear the words. They understand immediate family relationships.

Forty-three- to 48-month-olds are disobedient and independent, especially around their mothers. They love rhymes, can identify some colors, and know the names of body parts. They love whispered instructions, surprises, and secrets. They prefer to play alone but will play alongside other children.

Moral and Spiritual Development—Three-year-olds need to feel loved by adults. Show them special attention if they have younger brothers and sisters. Make them feel a part of the church group by making them "helpers." They can learn that God loves them, that God created them, that they are special to God, and that God helps them do many things. They learn moral and spiritual values by observing adults.

Development of Fours and Fives

Physical Development—Four- and five-year-old children use large muscles to climb on equipment, skip, move to music, and play classroom instruments. They use small muscles to draw and write with crayons, cut paper with blunt-nosed scissors, cut and paste, lace their shoes, button buttons, and wash their hands and faces.

Mental and Emotional Development—Four- and five-year-old children think literally. They can speak words that they do not understand; they learn by using their senses. They do not understand how other children feel or that they should share toys or instruments with them.

They like to imitate adults and role-play adult professions. They learn by playing. They like activities that make them feel big. Four-year-olds do not play in group situations as well as five-year-olds do.

Moral and Spiritual Development—Four- and five-year-olds are self-centered. They do not understand that other people have feelings or that they offend when they are loud and interrupt adults. Although they do not understand how to be considerate of others and share, they can begin to learn to share by taking turns when playing an instrument.

In choir, treat the children as you want to be treated. Do not discourage their ideas and input in activities. Help them understand which behaviors are appropriate in choir by rewarding and praising that which is acceptable and by not allowing that which is unacceptable.

Help them learn about God, Jesus, the Bible, the church, church music, themselves, others, their families, and the natural world through songs and activities in choir. Appropriate Bible thoughts to emphasize are found in *How to Guide Preschoolers*.*

Summary

No one really knows everything about a child's mental and emotional development in the womb, but the child does respond by moving when he hears loud noises or when the mother listens to certain types of loud music. Parents should prepare for the baby's arrival by singing the songs that they will sing to the child after he is born.

From birth, babies use their senses to learn. A proper foundation is laid for total development of the babies by showing love to them and practicing Christian values in the home. Parents should emphasize to young preschoolers that God loves them, Jesus loves them, and Jesus is their friend. Above all, remember that children develop morally and spiritually through adult example.

From 25 to 30 months, twos grow rapidly. They like to walk,

jump, tumble, run, climb, and pick up and throw objects. Because they are growing quickly, they are accident prone. Twenty-five- to 30-month-olds want to please adults but are afraid of strangers. They are self-centered and like to play alone instead of in groups. From 31 to 36 months, twos become selfish and disobedient, talk constantly, and like to say no. They are extremely ritualistic and want to be independent. They still do not understand the concept of sharing and need adult assistance in group activities. Thirty-one- to 36-month-olds are able to communicate verbally with care givers. They need to learn the difference between right and wrong and that some actions are improper.

Three-year-olds have better developed large muscle skills than small muscle skills. From 37 to 42 months, they can run easily, stand on one foot, climb a jungle gym, catch and throw a ball, and walk a straight line. From 43 to 48 months, their large muscle development allows them to tiptoe, hop, jump, and walk and run smoothly. From 37 to 42 months, children tend to be agreeable most of the time. Forty-three- to 48-month-olds are disobedient and independent, especially around their mothers.

Four- and five-year-old children think literally; they can speak words that they do not understand. They do not understand how other children feel or that they should share toys or instruments with them. Four-year-olds do not play in group situations as well as five-year-olds do.

Help them learn about God, Jesus, the Bible, the church, church music, themselves, others, their families, and the natural world through songs and other activities in choir.

Resources
How to Guide Preschoolers
Musical Experiences for Preschoolers; Birth Through Three
Understanding Today's Preschoolers

---

*Available at Baptist Book Stores or by calling toll free 1-800-458-BSSB.

2

Meeting the Special Needs
of Preschoolers

Children with handicapping conditions, children from non-English backgrounds, and children from troubled home situations have special needs that should be addressed and met by their music leaders. With the changing family structures in Anglo-American society in the last half of the 20th century, churches need to help children learn to deal with a variety of situations that they may encounter.

Exceptional Children

Handicapped, disabled, and exceptionally bright persons were misunderstood and mistreated for many years. However, with the passing of Public Law 94-142, The Education for All Handicapped Children Act, handicapped Americans have been guaranteed access to public schools since 1975. Additional legislation has made it possible for handicapped and disabled individuals to have access to barrier-free public facilities and to employment opportunities. Movies, such as *Rain Man*, and television programs, such as "Life Goes On," have heightened public awareness and understanding.

In your music activity groups and choirs, be sensitive to the needs of exceptional children. Exceptional children are those who are mentally handicapped, learning disabled, physically disabled, blind-visually handicapped, multihandicapped, or exceptionally bright.

Most exceptional preschoolers should be mainstreamed with regular preschoolers. By including them in regular music activities for preschoolers at church, these children have the opportunity to fully experience Christian education and nurture. Regular children in the music activity group or choir have the opportunity to learn about individual differences. They also have the opportunity to learn acceptance and appreciation of people who are "different."

As you seek to include exceptional children in music activity groups and choirs, enlist a leader who has experience, knowledge, or training with exceptional children. This leader can help plan individualized activities and adapt music activities to include *all* children. This leader can also adapt instruments for use by exceptional children. If no one in your church has experience working with exceptional children, read *Teaching Exceptional Persons*,* *Teaching Children and Youth with Mental Handicaps in Sunday School*,* and *Special Education Leadership* magazine.**

Language/Culture

Children are children. Whatever their language-cultural backgrounds, they need to be understood, accepted, and loved. Be aware of the cultural backgrounds of the children in your music activity group or choir. Avoid singing songs, planning activities, or making remarks that could possibly be offensive to one of them.

Language barriers between adult leaders and children arise in some parts of the United States because of the influx of non-English speaking persons, or because the majority of people in that area of the country are of different cultural origins. Learn basic communication skills with children. Know the specific words they use, whatever their background, to describe when they are hungry, thirsty, or need to use the toilet. If you are uncertain whether a child speaks English, ask the parents when the child first comes to music activity time or choir.

Family

Many American families are in crisis and turmoil today because of divorce, blended families, single parent families, death, and other problems. Because you may not always know

which children come from such situations, follow these princi-
ples in relating to each child in choir:
  • Recognize that a child's behavior can be a result of a family
crisis.
  • Love the child unconditionally.
  • Answer questions truthfully.
  • Help the child develop a positive self-image.
  • Help the child feel secure in music time or choir.
  • Speak on the child's level of understanding.
  • Provide both male and female role models in the music
group.

Divorced and Single Parent Families

Recognize that a large percentage of children come from di-
vorced homes. The ideal is for all children to experience a traditional family, but the reality is that many do not. In many
instances, no father is present in the home. In a growing number of instances, no mother is present. This is an important
reason to have both male and female leaders in each preschool
music group. Honestly answer questions that the children ask
about separation from a parent; be a special friend to the children and to the single parent with whom they live. Help the
children develop a healthy self-image. In family-focused activities, let each child decide who to include in his or her family
group so that someone will not have to say "I don't have a
daddy," or "I don't have a mother."

Blended Families

Younger preschoolers do not understand family relationships, and older preschoolers sometimes confuse those relationships. Help children in blended families understand that
their families are special and that they have many people who
love them. Give simple answers to their questions about members of the blended family. Give special care and preparation to
activities focusing on traditional family members. For example,
let the children suggest names to substitute in songs, such as
"Thank You, God, for Daddy."†

Death

Preschoolers do not understand death. They need careful and thoughtful guidance to avoid misconceptions about themselves and their family members regarding death. C. Sybil Waldrop, in *Understanding Today's Preschoolers,* * gives excellent counsel for dealing with preschoolers about death.

The child can accept death more easily than adults. He lives in the present, so he will not worry about tomorrow's reality. The preschool child has difficulty distinguishing between what is alive and what is inanimate. He thinks that a moving stone is alive and has feeling. It moves; therefore, it must be alive. Other things move—car, airplane. They, too, must be alive. The child cannot separate dreams, wishes, and imaginations from reality. A child needs to be assured that he cannot wish someone into dying. In a moment of anger or jealousy, a child may wish his parent would go away. If a parent were to die, the child might think he caused the person to die. Death then is difficult to explain to preschoolers who are limited in their thinking.

To young children, seeing is believing. The child can see the physical reality of death. The child can observe a dead bird to see that when something is dead, it is still. It does not eat. It stays dead. It does not become alive again. Death is not like sleep. When something sleeps, it wakes up. A child may be afraid to go to sleep if he associates sleep with death. Have you ever considered the frightening effects of the well-known bedtime prayer: "Now I lay me down to sleep; I pray the Lord my soul to keep. If I should die before I wake, I pray the Lord my soul to take"?

The child may equate separation with death. He may fear when a parent leaves that he or she will not return. For this reason, a child needs to hear that Mother or Daddy will come back. Parents can express the time of return in a tangible way. "Daddy will return after you and Mommy go to bed and wake up." Or Mother can leave a surprise package to open each day while she is away. "I will come back when all the packages are opened."

To assure the child that Mother or Daddy will not die soon, parents can explain that people usually live a long time and die when they are old.

To help a child during the death of a family member, friend, or pet, parents can:

1. Talk openly and honestly about their feelings. "Mother is sad because Grandmother died. I won't get to talk to her now."

2. Talk about the good memories of the person or pet.

3. Accept death as the last part of life and the portal to life eternal. The Christian's faith in life after death gives hope, comfort, and assurance. The child can sense the confidence and security with which his parents face death.[1]

Summary

Be sensitive to the needs of exceptional children. Exceptional children are those who are mentally handicapped, learning disabled, physically disabled, blind-visually handicapped, multi-handicapped, or exceptionally bright.

Learn basic communication skills with children. Know the specific words they use, whatever their background, to describe when they are hungry, thirsty, or need to use the toilet. Be aware of the cultural backgrounds of the children in your music activity group or choir.

Many American families today are impacted by divorce, death, turmoil, and other crises. Be aware of the fact that many children do not have a complete family unit living together. Younger preschoolers do not understand family relationships, and older preschoolers sometimes confuse those relationships. Help them feel loved and accepted.

Preschoolers do not understand death. Help them to feel secure and understand that death is a natural process. Preschoolers also need leaders to be caring and thoughtful about other problems their families face, such as unemployment, chronic illness, housing shortage, child-care issues, financial crises, and abusive situations.

---

[1]C. Sybil Waldrop, *Understanding Today's Preschoolers*, (Nashville: Convention Press, 1982), 138.

*Available at Baptist Book Stores or by calling toll free 1-800-458-BSSB.

**Available from the Customer Service Center, 127 Ninth Avenue, North, Nashville, Tennessee 37234, or by calling toll free 1-800-458-BSSB.

†Songs from *Musical Experiences for Preschoolers; Birth Through Three*.

3

Laying Spiritual Foundations

Through musical experiences preschoolers develop spiritual understandings of God, Jesus, the Bible, church, self, others, family, and the natural world.

Mention the names of God and Jesus frequently. Read stories from the Holman Read-to-Me Bible* and books from the Bible-and-Me Series* about God, Jesus, the Bible, church, self, others, family, and the natural world. Encourage preschoolers to participate in family devotion times and sing prayers to God. Select songs from *Musical Experiences for Preschoolers; Birth Through Three,** preschool song collections, and *The Music Leader*** that emphasize these spiritual understandings. Include these songs and the chanting of Bible thoughts in home and church activities. Use teaching pictures to help preschoolers visualize these spiritual understandings.

God

Birth Through Twos
- God is a name.
- God is a person.

25

Threes
- God is a person.
- God made earth and sky.
- God made plants and animals.
- God made people.
- God loves people.
- God wants people to love Him.
- People talk to God.
- God wants people to love one another.

Fours and Fives
- God is a person.
- God can do things people cannot do.
- God loves and cares for people.
- God wants people to thank Him.
- God wants people to worship Him.
- God wants people to learn about Him.

Jesus

Birth Through Twos
- Jesus is a name.
- Jesus is a person.
- Easter is a special day.

Threes
- Jesus was born.
- Jesus grew.
- Jesus had a family.
- Jesus helped people.
- Jesus loves people.
- Jesus wants people to love Him.
- Easter is a special day.

Fours and Fives
- Jesus was born.
- Jesus grew from a baby to a man.
- Jesus was a baby.
- Jesus was a boy.
- Jesus was a man.
- Jesus had a family.
- Jesus helped people because He loved them.

- Jesus loves me.
- Jesus loves others.
- Jesus wants people to love Him.
- Jesus is God's Son.
- Jesus can do many things people cannot do.
- Easter is a special day.

Bible

Birth Through Twos
- The Bible is an important book.

Threes
- The Bible is an important book.
- The Bible is a book about God and Jesus.

Fours and Fives
- The Bible is an important book.
- The Bible is a book about God and Jesus.
- The Bible helps people know how God wants them to live.
- The Bible has stories and verses about God, Jesus, and people.
- The Bible has stories about families who helped one another.

Church

Birth Through Twos
- People at church love me.
- People take care of me at the church building.
- People at the church building talk about God and Jesus.
- I use books, pictures, toys, and puzzles at the church building.

Threes
- People at church love me.
- I know other children and adults at church.
- People at church help others.
- I can help at church.
- People at church talk about God and Jesus.

Fours and Fives
- People at church love and care for me.

- I have friends at church.
- People at church help people who need help.
- I can help at church.
- People use the Bible at church.
- People at church sing songs, listen to Bible stories, and talk about God and Jesus.
- People at church have different tasks to do.
- People give money at church.
- People go to different church buildings.
- Going to church is important.

Self

Birth Through Twos
- I am a person.

Threes
- I am an important person.
- I am growing.
- I can do many things.

Fours and Fives
- I am important to God, self, and others.
- I am growing as God planned for me to grow.
- God wants me to take care of my body.
- I can think, work, and play because God gave me abilities.
- I can make some choices.
- I can take turns and share.

Others

Birth Through Twos
- I am aware of other people.
- People love me.
- People take care of my needs.

Threes
- Other people love me and care about me.
- Other people help me.
- I can love and help others.

Fours and Fives
- Certain people love and help me.

- God wants people to love and help each other.
- I can love and help others in many ways.
- People are alike in some ways and different in some ways.
- Each person has some rights.
- Some things belong to me, and some things belong to others.
- People have different kinds of work to do.
- God wants people to be friendly and have friends.

Family

Birth Through Twos
- I have a family.

Threes
- God planned for families.
- My family loves me.
- Other people are in my family.
- Family members help each other.
- I can help my family.

Fours and Fives
- God wants people to live, work, and play together in families.
- My family loves me.
- I am a member of a family.
- Family members help each other.
- I can help my family.
- Each family member has his own belongings and tasks to do.
- The Bible has stories about families who helped each other.

Natural World

Birth Through Twos
- I can discover what God made.
- I can use my senses to explore things God made.
- God made animals.

Threes
- God made earth and sky, plants and animals, and people.
- God provides food for people and animals.

Fours and Fives
- God made earth and sky; day and night; sun, moon, and stars; rain, snow, and wind; people; plants; animals; and things in the natural world.
- God wants people, plants, and animals to grow.
- God wants people to care for the things He made.

Summary
Through musical experiences, preschoolers develop spiritual understandings of God, Jesus, the Bible, church, self, others, family, and the natural world.

---

*Available at Baptist Book Stores or by calling toll free 1-800-458-BSSB.

**Available from the Customer Service Center, 127 Ninth Avenue, North, Nashville, Tennessee 37234, or by calling toll free 1-800-458-BSSB.

4

Laying Musical Foundations

Parents and leaders lay foundations for musical and spiritual growth in their preschoolers by involving them in musical activities at home and at church. Select activities from chapters 10, 13, and 16 which relate to the following musical responses at the different developmental levels:

Rhythm

Unborn
• Move when music is played.
Birth to Three Months
• Move in response to musical sound.
Three to Six Months
• Stop moving to turn toward the source of the musical sound.
Six to Nine Months
• Sway or move up and down after listening intently to music.
Nine to Twelve Months
• Remember simple motions to nursery songs.
Twelve to Eighteen Months
• Experience large movements to music.
• Vary movements to music.
• Use space when moving.
• Repeat some movements.
• Movements are not coordinated with music.
Eighteen to Twenty-four Months
• Dance to music with others.
• Move while singing.

- Attempt unsuccessfully to coordinate movements to the rhythm of the music.

Twos
- Move to music less than at an earlier age.
- Move after hearing many repetitions.
- Continue unsuccessfully at coordinating movements to the rhythm of the music.

Threes
- Use a variety of movements.
- Attempt unsuccessfully to coordinate movements to the rhythm of the music.
- Dance to music with others.

Fours and Fives
- Experience the steady beat.
- Experience sound and silence.
- Experience melodic rhythm (the rhythm of the words).

Pitch and Melody

Birth to Three Months
- Express feelings by crying.

Three to Six Months
- Begin to make babbling sounds.

Six to Nine Months
- Attempt to make vocal sounds after moving to music that is different from melodies and rhymes originally heard.
- Attempt to make vocal sounds before first attempts to speak.

Nine to Twelve Months
- Imitate vocal sounds.
- Imitate melodies.
- Cannot match pitches.

Twelve to Eighteen Months
- Attempt to sing short songs.
- Begin to imitate words of a song.

Eighteen to Twenty-four Months
- Continue to imitate words of a song.
- Sing spontaneously in everyday activities.
- Imitate rhythm and melodies of a song.

- Model singing after adults' singing.

Twos
- Continue to sing spontaneously.
- Sing alone.
- Sing more often than at an earlier age.
- Sing longer songs than at an earlier age.
- Learn songs by chanting words and rhythm.
- Range is from middle C to second-space A.
- Sing the G-E interval most often.

Threes
- Begin to sing correct words, rhythm, and melody.
- Invent new songs.
- Make new arrangements of familiar songs.
- Enjoy singing games.
- Enjoy imitating animal and environmental sounds in songs.
- Range is from middle C to second-space A.

Fours and Fives
- Find the singing voice through imitating a variety of sounds.
- Find the singing voice through singing conversation.
- Find the singing voice through singing alone in small and large groups.
- Range is from middle C to second-space A.
- Experience sounds that are same and different.
- Experience sounds that move up, down, and repeat.
- Experience sounds that are high and low.

Expression

Twos
- Respond to fast and slow.
- Respond to loud and soft.

Threes
- Respond to fast and slow.
- Respond to loud and soft.

Fours and Fives
- Respond to fast and slow.
- Respond to loud and soft.

- Experience a variety of moods through music.

Form

Fours and Fives
- Recognize same and different patterns and phrases in songs.

Harmony

Fours and Fives
- Experience songs acompanied by voices or other instruments.

Summary

Preschoolers enjoy music. They grow and develop through musical activities. Through experiencing musical activities at home and at church, they develop foundations for musical growth.

5

Laying Church Music Foundations

Through musical experiences, preschoolers develop the understanding that music is important in the worship and praise of God, in everyday living, in hymnody, and in outreach and missions.

Worship and Praise

- *Music helps people worship God at church, at home, or anyplace.*

Through musical activities at church and home, preschoolers learn that they can sing about God anytime and anywhere.

- *Music can be used to praise God.*

Preschoolers learn, through musical experiences, that they can praise God anywhere through music. Point out things in their environment for which they can be thankful.

- *Music helps a person talk to God.*

Preschoolers learn that they can talk to God through songs they sing, such as "God, We Thank You."†

- *Music helps a person express his feelings to God.*

Preschoolers can express their feelings to God by singing songs, such as "I Thank You, God."∞

- *Music helps a person learn about Jesus.*

"Jesus Was a Child," from the collection *I Like to Sing About Jesus,** helps preschoolers learn that Jesus was a baby, a boy, and a man and that He liked to help people.

- *Musical instruments help people praise God.*

Preschoolers can learn that they can use body instruments and other instruments to praise God.

Music in Everyday Living

• *Music helps families have a happy home.*

Music is an important part of preschoolers' routines at home. Sing songs about families. Sing hymn fragments and other songs as a part of family devotion time. Sing when the family travels or plays together.

• *Music is an important part of church activities.*

Preschoolers will know that music is an important part of church if they participate in music activities in music activity groups or choir, Sunday School, Discipleship Training, Mission Friends, worship services, and the nursery.

• *God gives people music to enjoy.*

Through enjoyable music activities at home and at church, preschoolers learn that God created music for people to enjoy.

• *Music helps make working and playing with others enjoyable.*

Through singing songs about being a helper and about playing with other children, preschoolers can learn that music can make work and play at home and at church enjoyable.

• *Music helps people learn of God's world.*

Preschoolers learn about their environment and God's creations by singing songs about God's world.

Hymnody

• *People write songs that others can sing to God.*

Preschoolers can learn that hymns are songs people can sing about God or to praise God in worship. People write songs that preschoolers can sing to God.

• *People can sing Bible verses and thoughts.*

Appropriate Bible verses and thoughts for younger and older preschoolers can be found in *How to Guide Preschoolers.* * Songs, such as "God Cares for You" † and "Children, Obey Your Parents," † are examples of Bible thoughts set to music and sung by preschoolers.

• *Hymns*

Choose carefully hymns and hymn fragments for preschoolers according to the appropriateness of text and range. Many hymn texts are not understandable by preschoolers, and the melodic ranges do not lie from middle C to A. The refrain of "There Is a Name I Love to Hear" (No. 66, *Baptist Hymnal*, 1975) or "Oh, How I Love Jesus," (No. 217, *The Baptist Hymnal*) is an example of an appropriate hymn fragment for preschoolers to sing.

Most hymn activities for preschoolers involve the hymn tune rather than the words. Hymn tunes can be used effectively at rest times, during transitional activities, and while preschoolers are playing freely in the block, home living, and book centers. Selections from *Hymns for Quiet Times** recording are appropriate for such activities. They also can be used for listening and moving activities.

The following hymns and hymn tunes are appropriate for preschoolers:

Christ the Lord Is Risen Today	EASTER HYMN
Come, Christians, Join to Sing	MADRID
Come, Thou Almighty King	ITALIAN HYMN
Fairest Lord Jesus	CRUSADER'S HYMN
For the Beauty of the Earth	DIX
I Love Thee	I LOVE THEE
Jesus Loves Me	CHINA
Jesus Shall Reign	DUKE STREET
Joy to the World! The Lord Is Come	ANTIOCH
Joyful, Joyful, We Adore Thee	HYMN TO JOY
Now Thank We All Our God	NUN DANKET
O Come, All Ye Faithful	ADESTE FIDELES
Oh, How I Love Jesus	OH, HOW I LOVE JESUS
Praise God, from Whom All Blessings Flow	OLD 100TH
Praise Him! Praise Him!	JOYFUL SONG
Praise the Lord! Ye Heavens, Adore Him	HYFRYDOL
Rejoice, Ye Pure in Heart	MARION
Stand Up and Bless the Lord	OLD 134TH
There Is a Name I Love to Hear	OH, HOW I LOVE JESUS
This Is My Father's World	TERRA PATRIS
We Gather Together	KREMSER
We Praise Thee, O God, Our Redeemer	KREMSER
When Morning Gilds the Skies	LAUDES DOMINI

Music in Outreach and Missions

• *Music is a way of telling others about Jesus.*

Preschoolers can tell their families and friends about Jesus by singing songs about Jesus for them. Preschoolers can tell their parents and other adult friends about Jesus when they visit music activity times at church and participate in music activities with them.

Summary

Through musical experiences, preschoolers develop the understanding that music is important in the worship and praise of God, in everyday living, in hymnody, and in outreach and missions.

---

*Available at Baptist Book Stores or by calling toll free 1-800-458-BSSB.
†Songs from *Musical Experiences for Preschoolers; Birth Through Three.*
ⁿⁿSongs from *Music for Today's Children.*

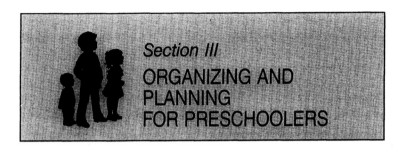

6

Organizing for Preschoolers

When organizing music groups and choirs for preschoolers, first consider the preschoolers. Make your plans in relationship to their needs. Babies, ones, twos, and threes have their needs. Fours have their set of needs, and fives have another set of needs. If rooms and trained leaders are available, plan to have separate groups or choirs for each age group. The leader-to-children ratio depends on the approach taken with the younger preschoolers. Parental involvement will reduce the number of leaders needed. Many preschool choirs for fours and fives function very well with one leader for every six preschoolers; however, one leader for every four preschoolers will assure preschoolers of individual attention.

Determining the potential number of preschoolers for music groups and choirs requires searching the church Sunday School rolls and at least estimating the number of prospects from the community. Once the potential number of children has been determined, a decision can be made concerning how many groups and choirs are needed.

Number of Choirs

Music activity groups can function with as few as two or three preschoolers, and choirs can function with as few as four or five preschoolers. Activity groups should be limited to 8 or 10 preschoolers, and choirs should be limited to no more than 18 on roll. More than the recommended maximum number presents a number of problems for the leaders and the children. Overcrowding diminishes the effectiveness and defeats the purpose of the activity group or choir. Keep in mind that the purpose is to lead preschoolers in developing spiritual and musical understandings and musical skills.

When an activity group or choir grows to exceed the maximum, divide it. The first logical division for groups would seem to be between ones and twos. The next logical division would seem to be between babies and ones and twos and threes, resulting in an activity group for each year.

The first logical division for preschool choirs is between fours and fives. Further division would be between younger fours and older fours and younger fives and older fives. However, the number of preschoolers in each age group has some bearing on the decision. Be flexible about where the division should come, for it may need to change from year to year. The number of trained leaders available definitely will influence the decision on grouping and grading. Use the grouping that works best for your church program, based on the current number of preschoolers, qualified leaders, and available space.

An option often overlooked is grouping five-year-olds and first graders together. First graders have unique needs, and fives are often nearer to first graders in skill and ability than to four-year-olds. Likewise, first graders are often nearer five-year-olds in skill development and maturity than to second and third graders. The reading skills of five-year-olds and first graders, too, often is at a similar level.

Number of Leaders

Music groups for younger preschoolers, birth through three, involving the parents and limiting the size of each group to eight families will require two leaders. Leaders needed for music groups not involving parents are as follows:

Babies—Ones	one leader for every child
Ones—Twos	one leader for every two children
Twos—Threes	one leader for every three children

An acceptable ratio for a preschool choir is one leader for every six four- and five-year-olds. The best ratio of leaders to preschoolers is one leader for every four four- and five-year-olds.

Time

The most significant question to answer in determining when preschool activity groups and choirs should meet is: *When can the most children be present?* If most of the preschoolers attend the church day care, the obvious time for activity groups or choirs is in conjunction with day care. If not, consider making the activity groups and choirs part of the Wednesday family night schedule. That is when most churches schedule music, missions, Sunday School preparation, and other training activities.

Talk with the parents. Are most of the mothers employed outside the home? A day activity group for children of nonworking mothers, and an early evening activity group for children of working mothers may be necessary to meet the needs of everyone.

How long should each activity group or choir meet?

The length of the weekly activity group or choir will need to be carefully considered. Fours and fives usually can handle 45-60 minutes. The time for threes and younger should be no more than 30 minutes.

Selecting Leaders

Master Potter

This child whose life I touch with mine
   Is like a piece of clay;
I take his gentle will in hand,
   And shape it day by day.

If I regard that God is love,
　　Then likely he will too,
Because this yielding piece of clay
　　Will pattern things I do.

If I respect my fellowman
　　And all his burdens share,
I'll find this young life being shaped
　　To love and really care.

The turns upon the wheel will shape
　　His habits, good and bad;
The edges rough and smooth are mine,
　　Upon this growing lad.

So thou who art the potter great,
　　Mold my life day by day;
That I, in turn, may shape this child
　　Whose life is trusting clay.[1]

Muriel Blackwell

Whatever we aspire to impart to preschoolers depends on the leader responsible for imparting the knowledge or developing skill. New learning should be presented in terms that children can understand. It must relate to what each child knows. Consequently, you must know and understand your preschoolers and curriculum materials thoroughly. Concentrate on each child's unique abilities. Guide your preschoolers to make discoveries about the new materials presented.

Concepts about music (learning) are formed in preschoolers' minds as a result of experiences in *doing* (making) music. For learning to take place, leaders must know preschoolers—how they learn, how they think, how they relate to adults and other preschoolers, what life is like at home, their physical abilities, their mental abilities, and their understandings about music.

Guide your preschoolers with care, love, understanding, and patience. Give the time necessary to help them make wonderful discoveries about music. These discoveries lead to learning, and learning leads to understanding. Help build foundations for a lifetime of musical understanding and expression. Preschoolers can be led to use music to praise God, witness to His great love, share the good news, and fellowship with other Christians with the foundations established by caring, loving leaders. Claim the implications in Deuteronomy 31:19-21:

> Now therefore write ye this song for you, and teach it the children of Israel: put it in their mouths, that this song may be a witness for me against the children of Israel. For when I shall have brought them into the land which I sware unto their fathers, that floweth with milk and honey; and they shall have eaten and filled themselves, and waxen fat; then will they turn unto other gods, and serve them, and provoke me, and break my covenant.
> And it shall come to pass, when many evils and troubles are befallen them, that this song shall testify against them as a witness; for it shall not be forgotten out of the mouths of their seed: for I know their imagination which they go about, even now, before I have brought them into the land which I sware.

You can know that ideas learned in a preschool music activity or choir are worth all the effort, training, preparation, and planning required for so great a challenge and responsibility.

Leader Qualifications

The qualifications of preschool music leaders are:
- Christian commitment
- Unconditional love of preschoolers
- Understanding of the growth and development of preschoolers
- Love of music
- Willingness to develop musical skills
- Pleasant singing voices and the ability to sing in tune

The most important qualification is Christian commitment. The ultimate purpose of a preschool music activity is to lay spiritual foundations and introduce preschoolers to Jesus as their very best friend—a friend who loves and cares for them all of the time.

An unconditional love for preschoolers is the second important qualification. Unconditional love requires time—time to care, time to visit, time to plan, time to train, time to practice new skills, and time to listen.

An understanding of the growth and development of preschoolers is another important qualification. This understanding need not come from someone with a degree in child psychology, although it could. This understanding comes from one who loves unconditionally and is willing to study the developmental process of preschoolers. This understanding comes to parents, guardians, care givers, and leaders from experiences with preschoolers.

The fourth qualification is the love of music. A leader cannot lead anyone to love, appreciate, and enjoy something which that leader does not love, appreciate, and enjoy.

Willingness to develop musical skills and leadership skills is an important qualification. The unconditional love of preschoolers compels leaders to strive to become better qualified.

A pleasant singing voice provides preschoolers a good model to hear and imitate. Imitation is one of the most important ways preschoolers learn. Singing in tune is critical when leading preschoolers to find their own singing voices and helping them learn to match pitch. Singing skills require practice and care of the voice. Develop your singing skills, use a pleasant voice when speaking and singing to your preschoolers, and always be mindful to sing in tune. Preschoolers deserve the best qualified leaders available, for this learning period is crucial for them. Foundations are established, skills developed, and concepts formed for a lifetime of response to God through music.

Leader Responsibilities

The responsibilities of leaders in a preschool music activity are:

Director—Responsible to the church music director or choir coordinator.

Responsibilities:

• Keep an updated profile on each enrolled preschooler's

physical, emotional, social, spiritual, and musical development.
- Plan and direct the activities.
- Lead in the planning of curriculum units and in the evaluation of the learning accomplished in each session.
- Guide the leaders.
- Coordinate the small-group activities and direct large-group activities.
- Plan for and direct appropriate sharing opportunities.
- Maintain communication with parents to inform them of various activities, and encourage the use of music in the home.
- Discover and enlist new members.
- Assist with music in other preschool organizations of the church.
- Develop an ongoing plan of personal growth.
- Serve on the Church Music Council in the absence of the choir coordinator.

Accompanist/Leader—The accompanist/leader assists the director, with primary responsibilities in accompanying.
Responsibilities:
- Provide accompaniment for large-group activities and sharing activities when needed.
- Assist the director in curriculum planning and in the evaluation of each unit.
- Assist in maintaining a profile for each preschooler.
- Plan and lead a small-group activity.
- Assist the director with large-group activities as needed.
- Participate in an ongoing plan of personal growth.

Other Leaders—Other leaders are responsible to the director.
Responsibilities:
- Assist the director in curriculum planning and in the evaluation of each unit.
- Assist in maintaining a profile for each preschooler.
- Plan and lead a small-group activity.
- Assist the director with large-group activities.
- Participate in an ongoing plan of personal growth.
- Assist in discovering and enlisting new members.
- Assist in providing social and recreational activities.

- Maintain attendance records, contact absentees, maintain music and study materials, coordinate transportation, assist with the room arrangement, assist in preparation of *Preschool Music Resource Kit*** items, assist in preparing items for parent communication, and serve as director in the director's absence.

Enlisting Leaders

The choir coordinator, director, or person responsible for leader enlistment should consider the following sources when looking for preschool music activity leaders:
- Parents of preschoolers
- Adult choir members
- Preschool leaders in other church program organizations
- School teachers
- Members of the congregation
- Youth choir members (if their schedules allow)
- Music director (if schedule allows)
- Men (preschoolers especially need the influence of male leaders)
- Music teachers (especially piano teachers)
- Church nursery workers
- Church day-care teachers

The process of enlisting leaders begins with observation. Look for people who display a love for and an understanding of preschoolers. Watch as the prospective leaders relate to preschoolers. Are their attitudes positive? Do they appear to enjoy talking with the preschoolers? Do they show consideration for preschoolers by stooping or sitting to talk with them on their eye level? Do the preschoolers appear to enjoy talking with and relating to the prospective leaders?

Before approaching anyone about leading preschoolers in musical experiences, give your observations thoughtful consideration, and make them a matter of prayer. After thinking and praying about those under consideration, give yourself a period of time to change your mind and to receive an answer to your prayers. When your list of prospective leaders is final, write a letter or make a phone call to the prospective leaders, asking for a personal visit.

At the time of the visit, explain the process through which you have arrived at this point. Give all the reasons why you think and feel that the person under consideration should lead preschoolers in musical experiences. Discuss each qualification, answering any questions the leader may have about responsibilities. If the prospective leader is agreeable, set a specific amount of time for him or her to consider and pray about all that you have shared. If, at the end of the specified time, you receive a negative answer, move on to the next prospect. If the answer is positive, proceed with the training process.

Training Leaders

Leader training should include the following steps:

Observation—the initial step. If observation is not possible at your church, make arrangements with another church in your city for your new leaders to observe their preschool music program.

Information—the study of this book and related curriculum materials.

Training—attendance at Church Music Week at the Ridgecrest or Glorieta Baptist Conference Centers, your state music week, or associational music conferences (usually held in late August or early September each year).

On-the-job Training—a period in which the newly-trained leader serves with an experienced preschool leader. The length of time will be determined by the number of trained leaders already in service and the needs of the preschoolers. This vital hands-on experience is the best possible way for newly-trained leaders to discover how preschoolers will respond to them.

Facilities

When the organization of activity groups and choirs has been completed and the process of enlisting and training leaders is underway, the next consideration is facilities, equipment, and supplies. Facilities will most likely be shared with other preschool organizations. To avoid conflict, talk with leaders of these other groups and determine practices and procedures for using the room. One workable solution is for everyone to be responsible for returning the room to a prearranged plan. The plan should be posted in the room and updated as needed.

Equipment

The curriculum units in *The Music Leader* are written for preschool music activity groups and choirs with the following instruments and equipment:
- Step bells
- Autoharp or ChromAharP
- Cassette player
- Record player (durable three-speed table model)
- Resonator bells
- Drums
- Triangles
- Finger cymbals
- Woodblocks
- Tone blocks
- Rhythm sticks
- Sand blocks
- Tambourines
- Wrist or loop bells
- Jingle bells
- Xylophones
- Piano

Optional:
- Other tuned and untuned percussion instruments

Nonmusical Equipment
- Chairs, some with seats 10 inches from the floor and some with seats 12 inches from the floor
- Tables, some 20 inches from the floor and some 22 inches from the floor. Number of each needed will be determined by the number of 10-inch and 12-inch chairs
- Tackboard or bulletin board

- Picture file
- Record player stand
- Wall supply cabinet
- Adult- and child-sized coatracks near the entrance
- Items that relate to the homeliving area

Using these lists or the "Equipment and Instrument Inventory" pages in *Preschool and Children's Choirs Plan Book*, inventory your materials and equipment to see what is available and what you need to purchase. Your church probably has money available through the church budget for equipment and supplies to use in the preschool room. Learn the process for requesting budget funds for the purchase of needed items.

Supplies and Materials

Supplies are expendable items, such as construction paper, crayons, felt-tip markers, newsprint, paint, and glue. Materials are the permanent items from the musical and nonmusical equipment lists. Before making budget requests, review the goals for the year, and determine your preschool music activity needs. Then, submit a list of needed supplies and materials, giving the sources of purchase and approximate prices.

Should your church not have money budgeted for the preschool activity groups and choirs, consider the following suggestions:

- Special offerings for specific needs
- Designated funds for music projects and equipment
- Special gifts from parents or grandparents

Often, funds are not available because the needs are not known.

Once materials and supplies are purchased, these items should be inventoried, put on a check-out-for-use system, and stored in the appropriate space provided by your church. Most churches have a place to store supplies that are used by all preschool organizations. In addition, a special resource area or room for musical equipment should be maintained by the Music Ministry. If you do not have a choir coordinator, you can find help in *Preschool and Children's Choirs Plan Book*.

Some teaching materials may be used again. Repeated use

constitutes good stewardship of church funds and time, and requires a filing system. The quarterly *Preschool Music Resource Kit* contains many such materials. Suggestions for filing these items are in the October issue each year.

Maintenance is also a part of good stewardship and a good example to set for preschoolers. Keep all equipment in good working order. Pianos need tuning at least once a year. Autoharps should be checked weekly for tuning. Provide a copy of the *ChromAharP Tuning Kit** for inexperienced leaders. Check record player needles often. Clean the tape player heads every six months.

Summary

Give the preschoolers first consideration when organizing music activity groups and choirs. Groups and choirs can function with as few as two or three or as many as 18 preschoolers. More than 18 in one group presents a number of problems for the leaders and the children. The ideal grouping is to have at least one choir or activity group for each age. Use the grouping that works best for your church program, based on the current number of preschoolers, qualified leaders, and available space. The best ratio of leaders to preschoolers in music activity groups is:

Babies—Ones	one leader for every child
Ones—Twos	one leader for every two children
Twos—Threes	one leader for every three children

An acceptable ratio for a preschool choir is one leader for every six four- and five-year-olds. The best ratio of leaders to preschoolers is one leader for every four four- and five-year-olds.

An option often overlooked when grading and grouping preschoolers is grouping five-year-olds and first graders together. First graders have unique needs, and five-year-olds are often nearer first graders in skill and ability than to four-year-olds. Likewise, first graders are often nearer five-year-olds in skill development and maturity than to second and third graders. The reading skill of five-year-olds and first graders often is at about the same level of proficiency.

The most significant question to answer in determining when an organization should meet is: *When can the most pre-*

schoolers be present? Each group and choir deserves special attention when planning the amount of time to be spent in musical experiences. New learning should be presented in terms that children can understand. For learning to take place, leaders must know preschoolers—how they learn, how they think, how they relate to adults and other preschoolers, what life is like at home, their physical abilities, their mental abilities, and their understandings about music. Concepts about music (learning) are formed in preschoolers' minds as a result of experiences in making (*doing*) music.

The most important leader qualification is Christian commitment. An unconditional love for preschoolers, an understanding of the growth and development of preschoolers, a love for music, and the willingness to develop musical and leading skills are also important leader qualifications.

[1]Muriel Blackwell, *Potter & Clay* (Nashville: Broadman Press, 1975), 17. Used by permission.

[2]From the *New Standard Bible.*© The Lockman Foundation, 1960, 1962, 1963, 1968, 1971, 1972, 1973, 1975, 1977. Used by permission.

*Available from Baptist Book Stores or by calling toll free 1-800-458-BSSB.

**Available from the Customer Service Center, 127 Ninth Avenue, North, Nashville, Tennessee 37234 or by calling toll free 1-800-458-BSSB.

7

Planning Musical Experiences for Preschoolers

Selecting and Using Curriculum Materials

Selecting curriculum materials to use in leading preschoolers in musical experiences is a critical decision. Planning is necessary to ensure that preschoolers' skills are developed and concepts formed in the proper sequence, building solid spiritual and musical foundations. The wide range of considerations due preschoolers, birth through age five, are numerous. The various levels of development from birth through five must be considered. These levels of development trace the motor skills, emotional relationships, intellectual skills, and spiritual concepts of the child. The developing child—his welfare and growth—should remain in the forefronts of our minds as we seek to establish solid foundations on which he can build and grow spiritually and musically in later years.

Choices of curriculum materials are many, different, and varied. Included among these choices are influences from Orff, Kodály, Dalcroze, and philosophies and methodologies from other influential music educators. Through the years, the curriculum writers for The Music Leader** have leaned heavily on these three methodologies as have the Broadman authors and composers. Everyday Rhythms for Children,* written by Susan Baker, is influenced by Dalcroze. Stepping Stones to Matching Tones,* written by Betty Bedsole and Derrell Billingsley, is based on the teachings of Orff and Kodály. The list could go on and on, for the shadows of these men fall across almost everything being done and offered in children's music education.[1]

The choice of curriculum materials for Southern Baptist

church music ministries should be those produced by the Church Music Department of the Baptist Sunday School Board. Every effort is made by the Church Music Department to keep up with the most effective teaching techniques and methods and incorporate these ideas into the curriculum materials. These dated curriculum materials help you follow the admonition of Lowell Mason in his *Elements of Vocal Music:* "The best teacher will not be confined to any particular previously laid out plan, but will from the different methods make out one of his own; not indeed one that is stereotyped and unalterable, but one that he may modify and adapt to the varying wants and circumstances of his different classes."[2]

"Know your boys and girls. Know their needs and how they learn best. Know what is available and how to apply it. Be the agent to bring the best teaching method to a particular learning style."[3] The units in *The Music Leader* and other curriculum materials produced by the Sunday School Board are based on spiritual objectives absent in other curriculum materials. Using these materials will remove the burden of remembering to include everything that is important for the preschoolers. The curriculum design includes development of spiritual and musical basic concepts and blends them appropriately with the preschoolers' total growth and development.

These materials may be ordered on the Church Literature Dated Form from the Customer Service Center, Baptist Sunday School Board, 127 Ninth Avenue, North, Nashville, Tennessee 37234 or from the Customer Service Center by calling toll free 1-800-458-BSSB.

The following list and brief description of each curriculum piece available for birth through age five should be helpful in guiding music leaders in making the selections needed.

A. *Musical Experiences for Preschoolers; Birth Through Three** is a 194-page book designed to aid music directors and other church musicians in making parents and other care givers aware of the importance of music in a child's development. It gives music leaders, parents, and care givers specific information about guiding younger preschoolers in musical activities. Each age level has a section of three chapters that details the development of preschoolers, supplies information about typical musical responses, and includes appropriate musical activities.

B. *Music for Threes*** is a resource kit containing 12 independent units of study in a 48-page booklet and 11 support items that include playscapes and characters, seasonal puzzles, a promotional poster, and a cassette containing all the music used in the units. *Music for Threes* is designed and written so leaders can provide preschoolers with both planned and spontaneous musical activities in listening, singing, moving, and creating music. Many of the activities require leaders to prepare and do most of the activity.

C. *The Music Leader*** is a 92-page quarterly magazine. *The Music Leader* is for leaders of preschool and children's choirs. It contains units of study (rehearsal procedures) for Preschool (four- and five-year-olds,) Younger Children's (grades 1-3,) Older Children's (grades 4-6,) and Grades 1-6 Choirs. There are also articles for leaders and choir coordinators, a special two-page "Music for Threes" feature, 10 pages of songs for preschoolers, and 14 pages divided into three units of study for preschoolers.

Each unit of study is written around a spiritual concept in one of the following areas: God, Jesus, the Bible, family, self, others, church, church music, and the natural world. Through musical experiences, preschoolers learn spiritual truths and develop understandings of and appropriate responses to rhythm, melody, form, expression, and harmony.

Study a preschool unit in a current issue of *The Music Leader*. You will find the following:

• Title—The title of the unit grows out of the spiritual goal for the unit. The unit song and many of the activities in the unit relate to the theme title.

• Weeks—Each unit is one month in length. The number of weeks in a unit is determined by the number of Wednesdays in the month since most preschool music activities meet on Wednesdays. If your meeting time is another day, you may need to adapt your schedule by either starting a unit a few days before the first of the month or running a day or two into the next month.

• Unit Song—The unit song undergirds and reinforces the unit theme and spiritual goal. It is the basis for many learning experiences in which the preschoolers can achieve the musical goals for the unit. The unit song is published in *The Music Leader* and is recorded on the quarterly *Preschool Music Cassette*** and *Preschool Music Recording.***

• Goals—Goals are based on the spiritual and musical foundations discussed in detail in chapters 3-5 of this book. Each unit is built around one spiritual goal and five musical goals. The musical goals relate to rhythm, melody, form, expression, and harmony. The form and harmony goals are always the same. The rhythm, melody, and expression goals are taken from the preschool and children's musical development chart. The preschool section of this chart appears on pages 214-218.

• Music and Materials—The songs for each unit in *The Music Leader* are listed in the contents of each unit by title and page number. *(PMC/PMR)* appears by each song title recorded on the *Preschool Music Cassette/Preschool Music Recording.* Songs that are in *The Music Leader* are followed by a list of songs from other resources that are used in the unit. Recordings and other teaching materials are listed last. Checking the list early in your preparation time will help you determine the materials you need for each unit.

• Preparation for the Unit—This section offers time-saving suggestions for gathering materials, planning, and teaching the unit. It enables you to plan ahead by giving information about items that take time to prepare or need to be purchased.

• Activities—Several activities for use in small groups follow "Preparation for the Unit." Each activity is designed to help achieve a specific goal. The activities are listed in the same order as the goals to which they relate. Some activities may relate to the same goal, but each will have a different purpose. If you do not use a suggested activity, be sure that the activity you substitute will achieve the same purpose as the one replaced.

• Weekly rehearsal procedures—These procedures follow the listing of activities. Specific small-group activities are suggested for each week, followed by a suggested plan for the large group. The activities in the large-group plans are sequenced

We Are Friends

by BARBARA SANDERS

Happy Times with Friends at Church, page 43

I Have a Friend, page 41 *(PMC/PMR)*

I Went to Visit a Friend, page 42

A Song Just Comes Out, page 37 *(PMC/PMR)*

Thank You, God, for Jesus, page 40

Thanksgiving Day, page 39

*Preschool Music Resource Kit (PMRK), 10/90

Thank You, God, for Friends, Item 7

**Baptist Hymnal, 1975 (BH)

We Gather Together, No. 229

MATERIALS

*Music Time (MT), 10/90

*Preschool Music Cassette (PMC), 10/90

*Preschool Music Recording (PMR), 10/90

*Preschool Music Resource Kit (PMRK), 10/90

Side 1 of PMC contains the same music as PMR (with voices and accompaniment). Side 2 of the cassette contains accompaniment only.

*Order on Church Literature Dated Form.
**Available at Baptist Book Stores.

PRESCHOOL CHOIR
NOVEMBER UNIT
(Four Weeks)

UNIT SONG: "I Have a Friend"

GOALS

Spiritual Development—Preschoolers will come to understand that God wants everyone to love and help one another.

Musical Understanding—Preschoolers will come to understand that pitches are high or low and that melodies have long and short sounds and can express different kinds of feelings.

Skill Development—Preschoolers will develop their singing and moving skills as they acquire musical understanding through participation in singing and moving experiences.

MUSIC

*The Music Leader (TML), 10/90

Christmas Tells of Jesus, page 44 *(PMC/PMR)*

PREPARATION FOR THE UNIT

Make a "Singing Skills/Attendance Check-in Chart" to use each week by drawing horizontal lines two inches apart on poster paper. Divide the poster into five vertical columns. Place each preschooler's name on a line in the left column under the heading "Name." Include these headings for the four remaining columns: Column 2, Week 1—Responded "I am here," using my singing voice. Column 3, Week 2—Measured "How tall I am" for good singing posture. Column 4, Week 3—Used a long breath to blow a pinwheel. Column 5, Week 4—Matched a pitch. Use stickers to mark attendance for columns 2, 4, and 5. Record height in column 3.

Name	Singing Voice	Singing Posture	Breath Control	Matching Pitch
Angela				
Christy				
David				
Erin				
Jamy				
Jeremy				
Mark				
Paul				
Rachel				

to Psalm 139:14 and read, "God made me." Say: "God made us with mouths that can sing. What else can our mouths do?" Guide children to respond until someone answers, "Eat."

4. Display Item 1, *PMRK*, and point to the carrot and honey pictures in stanza 4. Say, "These are things we can eat." Ask the children to play steady beats on their lap drums as you chant stanza 4 of "All These Things." Chant the rhythm of the words as you point to the corresponding pictures.

5. Have children stop playing their lap drums. Echo chant stanza 4 with them. Then echo sing stanza 4.

6. Open a Bible to 1 Peter 5:7 and read, "God cares for you." Say, "Today you played a song about God's care."

7. Sing "God Cares for You." As you sing, show the melodic movement by tapping your head with your hands for each G pitch and tapping your shoulders for each E pitch. Sing very slowly. Then ask the group to stand, sing, and do the same up and down arm movements.

8. Seat the preschoolers. Let a child play the *ostinato* as everyone sings "God Cares for You" again. Thank God for making and caring for every person.

9. Play "We Gather Together" *(PMC/PMR)* as you distribute *Music Time*, Week 1.

WEEK 2
SMALL GROUPS
Suggested Activities: D, E, and F
LARGE GROUP
1. Repeat Week 1, Step 1. Chant stanzas 1 and 2.

2. Play "A Song Just Comes Out" *(PMC/PMR*, Version 1) and display Items 2a-b, *PMRK*. Have the leader of Activity D point to the correct blocks on the song map as you lead the children to move as in Activity D.

3. Seat everyone. Have the preschoolers sing stanzas 1 and 2 of "A Song Just Comes Out" as you point to the song map.

4. Ask the children to look at the song map. Tell them to find the two parts of the song that are alike. Have one child go to the song map and touch the identical

parts.

5. Refer to the story that was read in Activity E. Say: "Let's pretend we are up in the tree house with Ashley and Chuck. Look around. Tell me what you see." Guide the children to respond until they name *flowers, trees,* and *grass.* Say: "That's right! Let's listen to a song about things we can see."

6. As the children listen to stanza 1 of "All These Things" *(PMC/PMR)*, point to Item 1, *PMRK*. Sing stanza 1 together. Say, "When I sing about flowers and grass, I think of something God says."

7. Open a Bible to Matthew 6:28-30 and add, "God takes good care of flowers and grass and He cares about us even more. Let's sing 'God Cares for You.'" Let a child play the *ostinato* as *all* sing.

8. Ask the group to stand, sing, and move as in Week 1, Step 7. Say: "God really does care for us. He also loves us." Read "God loves us" (1 John 4:10) from the Bible.

9. Echo sing stanza 1 of "I Know." Thank God for loving every person.

10. Play "We Gather Together" *(PMC/PMR)* and distribute *Music Time*, Week 2.

WEEK 3
SMALL GROUPS
Suggested Activities: G, H, and I
LARGE GROUP
1. Whisper to each small group: "Go to large group like birds. Flap your wings and softly sing 'tweet, tweet.'" Play "We Gather Together" *(PMC/PMR)* as the children assemble. Say, "Listen to two different ways this hymn sounds." Discuss the differences. (Different instruments, tempos, and moods.)

2. Say: "We used our ears to listen to that hymn. One of our songs tells about our ears." Using Item 1, *PMRK*, echo chant stanza 2 of "All These Things." Chant once softly and once loudly.

3. Have the children sing stanzas 1 and 2 with *PMC/PMR*. With piano or Autoharp accompaniment, have them sing stanzas 1 and 2 again.

4. Say, "Singing about birds reminds me of what the Bible says." Open a Bible to Matthew 6:26 and say, "Jesus says that

numerically and begin with action verbs in boldface type. These activities, like the small-group activities, may need to be adapted for your preschoolers.

As you consider the units, keep your preschoolers' needs in mind. Also, keep in mind your financial limitations and your personal strengths and weaknesses. Adapt units to meet your specific situations. When changes are necessary, replace one activity with an activity that has the same purpose. Otherwise, the children may grow in some areas and remain undernourished in other areas.

D. *Music Time (MT)*** is a four-page leaflet for preschoolers to take home from choir each week. It contains songs, poems, chants, stories, activities, and notes to parents. *Music Time* is written by the curriculum writers for *The Music Leader* and is designed to extend the musical experiences into the home. The content is directly related to the content of the unit materials in *The Music Leader.*

E. *Preschool Music Resource Kit (PMRK)*** is a package of teaching aids, such as pictures, musical games, song posters, puzzles, patterns, charts, and filmslips. *Preschool Music Resource Kit* minimizes leader preparation time and maximizes leader effectiveness. The content is directly related to unit ma-

Preschool Music Resource Kit

For Preschool Choir Leaders

October, November, December 1989

Volume 11, Number 1

The materials in this kit implement the teaching suggestions found in the preschool units of the October, November, December 1989 issue of *The Music Leader.* Use of the kit will make learning experiences more meaningful and interesting for your four- and five-year-olds in Preschool choir. The prepared materials will also help save valuable preparation time for leaders.

CONTENTS

OCTOBER: LOVE ONE ANOTHER
Items 1a-b.   Friendship Hill Gameboard, Playing Pieces, and Game Cards
Item 2.   Spin, Say, and Play Gameboard
Item 3.   Strong/Weak Drum Chart
Item 4.   Helpers Concentration Game
Item 5.   Bragging Bracelets

NOVEMBER: GOD LOVES ME
Items 6a-b.   High/Low Spider Gameboard and High/Low Spider
Item 7.   Feelings Gameboard and Spinner
Items 8a-d .   Thanksgiving Story Pictures
Item 9.   Long/Short Feather Pattern
Item 10.   "God Made Me and He Loves Me" Autoharp Card
Item 11.   "I See You, Little Spider" Motion Card
Item 12.   Thanksgiving Story

DECEMBER: IT'S CHRISTMAS!
Item 13.   "Popcorn" Song Chart
Items 14a-b.   Trip to Bethlehem Fast/Slow Chart and Donkey
Item 15.   "Why It's Christmas" Bell *Ostinato*
Items 16a-b.   Jesus' Baby Book and Add-on Pictures
Item 17.   "Away in a Manger" Autoharp Card

terials found in *The Music Leader, Music Time*, and *Preschool Music Cassette/Preschool Music Recording.* Some pieces from the kit can be covered with clear, adhesive-backed plastic paper and saved for future use. Preschoolers like to use favorite items again and again.

F. *Preschool Music Cassette (PMC)*** is a two-sided cassette tape of songs and listening activities from the preschool units. The cassette may be used in leader preparation, small-group activities, and large-group activities. Side 1 of *PMC* contains the same music as *PMR* with voices and accompaniment. Side 2 of the cassette contains accompaniment only.

G. *Preschool Music Recording (PMR)*** is a seven-inch, 33⅓ rpm recording of songs and listening activities from the preschool unit. The recording may be used in leader preparation, small-group activities, and large-group activities.[4]

The Planning Meeting

Planning for preschool choir is imperative if the children are to develop spiritually and musically. Directors must first know what they expect to accomplish in preschool choir, then communicate their expectations to the leaders. Leaders need time to prepare so they can feel confident in the material they present. Planning can be done monthly, one week prior to the beginning of the new unit, or quarterly, soon after the new literature order arrives. The planning process occurs in three stages.

• *Stage 1*—Study all the new materials, listen to the recordings or cassettes, and examine the items in the *Preschool Music Resource Kit*. Make notes as to which activities can best be used with the preschoolers in your choir. Consider the amount of time your choir meets, the amount of space you have, the number of preschoolers you have, and the age and developmental level of those preschoolers.

• *Stage 2*—Give the leaders copies of *The Music Leader* with marked notations regarding specific activities to read and reminders of the date and time of the planning meeting. The leaders should receive *The Music Leader* at least one week before the scheduled planning meeting so they will have enough time to become familiar with the unit.

• *Stage 3*—Begin the planning meeting with prayer for guidance and understanding. Review and evaluate the previous unit. Learn from your leaders which activities worked well and which ones did not. Talk about specific problems and needs of your preschoolers. Discuss the learning progress of each preschooler and make written notations.

Make note of any special plans for the month, such as parent visitation night or birthday recognitions. Sing through all of the songs from *The Music Leader* that will be used in the unit. Plan to commit the songs to memory before choir time. Thoroughly discuss the goals and specific plans for each leader. Use the planning charts in the annual *Preschool and Children's Choirs Plan Book* to facilitate the planning session. Keep complete notes of your plans. Give everyone in attendance a copy of the plans for the unit. An added advantage to having the plans written is for those times when a substitute might be needed for one of your leaders.

When all leaders know what is expected of them each week, they will proceed with confidence and effectiveness.

Summary

Selecting curriculum materials to use in leading preschoolers in musical experiences is critical. The choice of curriculum materials for Southern Baptist church music ministries should be those produced by the Church Music Department of the Baptist Sunday School Board. Using these materials will remove the burden of remembering to include everything that is important for the preschoolers.

Planning for preschool choir is imperative if the children are to develop spiritually and musically.

---

[1]Veteria (Tee) Billingsley, "What's In a Name?" *The Music Leader*, April-June 1990, 20.
[2]Lowell Mason, *Elements of Vocal Music.*
[3]Billingsley, "What's in a Name?" p. 20.
[4]Based on material from Betty Bedsole, Derrell Billingsley, and G. Ronald Jackson, *Leading Preschool Choirs* (Nashville: Convention Press, 1985), 102-104.
*Available from Baptist Book Stores or by calling toll free 1-800-458-BSSB.
**Available from the Customer Service Center, 127 Ninth Avenue, North, Nashville, Tennessee 37234, or by calling toll free 1-800-458-BSSB.

8

Enlisting Preschoolers

"Look all the world over, there's no one like me."[1]
"Special, special, I am very special, God made me that way."[2]
These are opening lines from two preschool songs about how special each child is to his family and to God. People are unique and possess special qualities. God did not make any two people alike. Preschoolers need to learn this truth. Each must feel that he is a person of worth. Children depend on adults to help them develop a positive sense of self-worth. Caring adults have the responsibility to choose the proper learning experiences and to provide a safe learning environment for preschoolers. At no other time in their lives will they learn so much in such a short time span. The critical preschool years determine how pre-schoolers learn and accept new ideas for the rest of their lives. Music can help set the stage for future learning, making pre-school music activities especially important during these for-mative years of acquiring knowledge. Preschoolers need musical experiences to establish strong musical foundations. For many preschoolers, music activity time will be their first exposure to church music and spiritual concepts. Exposing preschoolers to the proper learning environment is no small task. Many people are involved in the process.

Involving the Church

The church music director or choir coordinator makes plans to train leaders. The church staff or Church Council coordi-nates schedules with other church activities, maintains the rooms, orders the supplies and curriculum materials, and plans the budget to include the needs of the children's choir leaders.

How are leaders involved? Leaders train and keep up with the latest in music teaching methods, materials, and ideas. Leaders spend a lot of time in planning and preparation for each week's activity time, assisting the director in outreach and creating an atmosphere in which children will want to be a part of the music activities.

Involving the Family

Parents have the responsibility of seeing that preschoolers attend music activity time. This is not an easy task. Cooperation of the entire family is necessary. Getting preschoolers to music activity time is not enough. Parents also must see that preschoolers arrive in a good mood and are fed, rested, and ready for learning experiences.

Involving the Preschooler

Preschoolers often come to music activity time from a day-care center and would rather go home and be with the family or play with their own toys. Learning takes energy, and sometimes preschoolers are asked to exert more learning energy at the end of a busy day when they have none left.

The task the church faces in providing a music activity time is intense when put in this perspective. Learning experiences for preschoolers do not *just happen*. Preschoolers do not show up at the door of the room at the appointed time without a strong effort on the part of caring parents and other caring adults. The church needs a strong planned outreach program to locate, contact, and communicate with preschoolers and their families to get preschoolers to this important learning opportunity.

Locating preschoolers and their families may be the easiest of the church's responsibilities. Look first to the Sunday School rolls and plan to involve all preschoolers who are already associated with the church. Look at the church prospect lists and contact families who have preschoolers. The Young Married Couples Sunday School Department usually has families with babies from birth through age two who will soon be ready for a preschool music activity. Educate, inform, and encourage these parents to bring their preschoolers to the music activity time. Most parents are interested in seeing that their children have the best of everything. They will likely be interested in what the church can provide for their children. Give them suggestions for musical activities at home. Introduce them to *Musical Experiences for Preschoolers; Birth Through Three.** Look to the community around your church and send publicity to day-care centers. Expect your enrollment to increase when you have expended this effort. Providing adequate space and leadership is the responsibility of the church. Communicate your needs to your music director.

Specific helps for publicity and promotion are offered periodically in *The Music Leader.*** Other sources for publicity and promotion ideas include *Promo Ideas for Preschool and Children's Choirs,*** and *The Choir Coordinator's Notebook.** Keep in mind that the target group for your promotion is parents of preschoolers. The most effective means of reaching the parents is through personal home visitation. Promote preschool music activity through church newsletters, cards, and phone calls. Increase the effectiveness of publicity efforts by strategically placing posters and other visuals so parents will see them. Whatever approach taken to promotion and publicity, the key to success is consistency and follow-through.

Select a theme and use it for a year. A theme gives an identity to all mail and publicity related to the Music Ministry of your church. Provide everyone a variety of art work and logos to use throughout the year on letterheads, bulletin inserts, church newsletters, and take-home pieces for the children.

A personal letter from the music director of your church to the parents of preschoolers is an effective way to give information regarding opportunities preschool music activities afford preschoolers. Inclusion of specific types of information preschoolers will learn during the preschool music activity time is helpful. Today's parents usually are aware of good educational methods and will benefit in knowing that those methods are used during a preschool music activity.

A periodic visit to the opening assembly of the Young Married Couples Sunday School Department with a brief presentation of the value of church music education for preschoolers is a way to stay in touch. Be visible to the parents of preschoolers. Encourage them to ask questions. The more parents know, the more they will tend to see that their preschoolers attend. Be aggressive in your publicity and promotion.

Records

Equally as important as making the contact and enlisting preschoolers and their families is keeping track of them. Record keeping is the only way to maintain a viable communication channel through which ministry can flow. Records on each preschooler should be maintained. When new babies arrive in church, someone representing the Music Ministry should be among the first to welcome these prospective singers. The records should travel with the children as they progress through the various programs through the years. Each new group of leaders will benefit from knowing what the children have learned.

Individual Records—Use the Music Ministry Enrollment Card, Form CM1, BBS #4383-13, to enroll your boys and girls.

The Music Ministry Individual Attendance Record, Form CM2A, BBS #4383-14, contains essential information about the preschooler and his record of attendance for one year. If you choose this type of record system, keep each member's card together in a notebook. One leader in your choir should be responsible for maintaining this record system.

Use the Music Ministry Individual Information Sheet, Form CM5, BBS #4383-90, to gather more detailed information on each preschooler. Keep it in a permanent file in the church music director's office and update it annually.

Make a choir prospect card to keep important information on preschoolers who are prospective choir members. The card should contain the prospect's name, address, phone number, his parents' names, business address, business phone number, and the preschooler's age. Fill out this card on each preschooler when new families join the church. Visit in the home and encourage the parents to bring their preschooler to choir.

Group Records—The Music Ministry Weekly Attendance Record, Form CM3, BBS #4383-16, is an alternative for the Music Ministry Individual Attendance Record. You do not need to use both forms. Choose the one that best fits your needs.

The Music Ministry Weekly Attendance Record can be used to compile information from the individual records in a form that becomes the weekly report. This information is then transferred to the monthly report. If you use the alternative Music Ministry Group Attendance Record form, there is no need for this one.

The church music director's office completes the Music Ministry Report Book, Form CM4, BBS #4383-17, using information furnished by your choir. It contains the information for making a report to the church in the monthly business meeting and in preparing the annual associational letter.

Leadership Records—It will be helpful to record the attendance of each leader, either by using a Music Ministry Individual Attendance Record form or by listing all the leaders from your choir on the Music Ministry Group Attendance Record form. The form you use will depend on the record system that you decide on for your choir.

A leadership directory with names, addresses, and telephone numbers will be helpful to you and your choir leaders. This type directory is included in the annual *Preschool and Children's Choirs Plan Book*.

Keep a Music Ministry Individual Information Sheet on each choir leader. Use this sheet to record their music and nonmusical interests; that will be helpful when planning special projects. Keep these forms filed in the church music director's office. Sometimes family history exists, history that has a direct bearing on the way a child behaves in a given circumstance, and leaders who know these facts can be more effective. For example, a three-year-old receives a new sibling into the family in a much different way than a second grader. If a grandparent comes to live in the home, a preschooler may express his change in living arrangements in some behavioral way during group learning times. Unless adequate records are kept and updated during the year, developments may occur that escape the attention of the preschool music activity leader.

Who is responsible for keeping these extensive records? The responsibility lies in all departments of the Music Ministry. The choir coordinator should supply information to the preschool music activity group or choir director. The director should see that such material is recorded on the individual record chart. Leaders involved with preschoolers will learn about events each week that occur in the lives of preschoolers. Is there a new sibling due? Does the child have a new pet? Is there an expected change in where the child will be living? Is someone ill? Will the child be starting in a day-care program because Mother is going to work outside the home? Information should be placed on the individual record chart and shared among leaders. Having this information will offer the leaders opportunities to know how to pray for the children and how to minister to their families.

Monthly planning meetings should be times of review and updating the individual record of each preschooler. If done on a monthly basis, the upkeep of the records should take only a minimum of time. If left to one person to record all the events of a quarter, the job can become enormous.

Sometimes the only adequate way to maintain consistent record keeping for a group is to divide the work load among the leaders. Let one leader be responsible for a small group of children for a period of one year. Another way to divide the work load is by job assignment.

- Assign one leader to keep the attendance records weekly.
- Assign one leader to contact all absentees. When children are ill, the leader is responsible for sending get well cards and contacting the parents to see if other types of visits and phone calls are needed.
- Assign one leader the responsibility of ministering by sending birthday cards or making birthday visits.

Preschoolers enjoy seeing their leaders outside of the usual setting. Preschoolers are possessive about their leaders and will benefit from the home visit and personal phone call.

Other types of information about preschoolers help future leaders in planning for continued learning experiences. If a child does not find his singing voice before moving into younger children's choir, perhaps a problem exists that the parent needs to know about. Sometimes hearing difficulties can be discovered first by music leaders. Sometimes maturity levels have not advanced according to the chronological age. Parents and future music leaders should be aware of these problems. The level of understanding that a preschooler develops by age five should include hearing the difference in high and low pitches and matching pitches within a limited range. If this does not happen, the director of the first-grade choir should be made aware of that at the beginning of the music year.

Summary

Preschoolers need to feel that they are persons of worth. They depend on adults to help them develop a positive sense of self-worth.

Effective preschool music activities require the involvement of the church family and staff, the preschooler's family, and the preschooler. The church music director or choir coordinator makes plans to train leaders. Leaders train and keep up with the latest in music teaching methods, materials, and ideas. Parents see that preschoolers attend music activity time, and preschoolers are asked to exert more learning energy at the end of a busy day when, sometimes, they have none left. The task the church faces in providing a music activity time is intense when put in this perspective. Learning experiences for preschoolers do not *just happen.*

The church needs a strong planned outreach program to locate, contact, and communicate with preschoolers and their families to make them aware of this important learning opportunity.

1Trilby Jordan, "There's No One Exactly Like Me." © Copyright 1975 Broadman Press (SESAC). All rights reserved. International copyright secured. Used by permission.

2Derrell Billingsley, "I Am Very Special." © Copyright 1977 Broadman Press (SESAC). All rights reserved. International copyright secured. Used by permission.

*Available at Baptist Book Stores or by calling toll free 1-800-458-BSSB.

**Available from the Customer Service Center, 127 Ninth Avenue, North, Nashville, Tennessee 37234, or by calling toll free 1-800-458-BSSB.

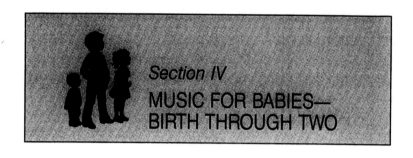

9

Preparing Musical Activities for Babies, Ones, and Twos

Enlisting Leaders

Enlisting effective leaders is an important element in leading preschoolers in musical activities. Adults who love children, love God, love music, and are willing to learn about how babies, ones, and twos learn are candidates for leading preschoolers in musical activities. A discussion of leadership qualifications is included in this chapter. You can find potential leaders among parents of the children, Sunday School and Discipleship Training teachers, extended session workers, daycare center teachers, adult choir members, single adults, and senior adults.

Number of Leaders

The number of children you anticipate in a music activity group will determine the number of adult leaders you need. An ideal situation is to invite parents to participate with their children in musical activities. If this ideal is unattainable, two adult leaders for a group of five or six children is sufficient. With larger groups, one additional adult for every four or five children is helpful. Smaller rooms are more suitable for younger preschoolers than for fours and fives because younger preschoolers require less space for large-group activities. They prefer individual and small-group activities. A music activity group with a maximum of eight families (8 × 1 child + 1 parent = 16) or 12 younger preschoolers and three adult leaders is recommended. You will need to decide if you wish to combine birth- through one-year-olds with two- and three-year-olds. The number of prospective children and parents, the number of qualified leaders, adequate space, proper equipment, and interest are some of the determinates involved in the decision.

Leader Qualifications

After deciding on the number of leaders you need, search for leaders who meet the qualifications for leading music activities for babies, ones, and twos. Being a professing Christian is the most important qualification because one of the ways children learn about God's love and Jesus' love is through seeing it lived in the lives of the leaders with whom they interact. Unsaved leaders cannot share something they do not have. Leaders must love preschoolers, for the preschoolers will feel this love, and it will help them develop positive concepts and attitudes about themselves, others, God, Jesus, the Bible, church, their families, the natural world, and church music. Love is shown through kindness and patience, especially with twos.

Acquiring an understanding of how babies, ones, and twos develop is necessary to work effectively with them. Leading younger preschoolers is quite different from leading children, youth, and adults. *Understanding Today's Preschoolers** and *Guiding Your Child Toward God** by C. Sybil Waldrop, and *Musical Experiences for Preschoolers; Birth Through Three** by Rhonda Edge will help adults understand the physical, mental and emotional, spiritual, and musical development of preschoolers from birth through age two.

A love for and a basic understanding of music is helpful.

Singing in tune with a light voice is important because younger preschoolers learn how to sing in tune by listening to adults sing to them. Volunteers can be trained to be good music leaders.

The Role of Leaders

The role of leaders in musical activities for babies through twos is different than that for leaders of fours and fives, requiring active participation on an "as needed" basis. Provide a musical environment, and let the children's interest and curiosity dictate the course of musical exploration and discovery. Create the setting for learning to take place without consciously trying to teach the specific musical concepts that fours and fives normally learn. Do finger plays and sing nursery rhymes, singing games, and songs about church to the children. Play recordings, set up learning centers (for twos), provide musical manipulatives and crib toys, and sing spontaneously while watching the children play. Be flexible and sensitive to the needs and interests of the children. An effective preschool leader follows their interests and curiosity and allows the questions to be formed in their minds before supplying the answers. Curiosity leads to discovery. Provide materials that will stimulate preschoolers' curiosity and cause them to ask questions. Be slow to teach and quick to let preschoolers discover.

Potential Places for Musical Activities

Music is an important part of the environment of babies, ones, and twos, so musical experiences should be encouraged in younger preschoolers' homes and in all their experiences at church. The most important experiences take place in the home, and music is no exception. Younger preschoolers' musical growth and the music they like are shaped largely by the home environment; therefore, music should be included in daily routines and should be shared by the families.

The church nursery affords babies, ones, and twos the opportunity to equate coming to church with happy feelings. Because younger preschoolers relate easily to music, preschool leaders in all church program organizations should use music as a medium for promoting their moral and spiritual development. Activities, such as rocking and singing to babies, playing recordings of hymns while ones play, and singing songs for twos that relate to books in the Bible-and-Me Series,* contribute significantly to their moral and spiritual development.

Songs that emphasize God, Jesus, the Bible, church, church music, self, others, the natural world, and family are used effectively in Sunday School to help illustrate Bible stories and thoughts with twos. The rhyming words in many children's songs are attractive to younger preschoolers and help them enjoy hearing the stories and songs repeatedly.

Use Discipleship Training as a time for parents and their babies, ones, and twos to share musical activities together. Coupled with information about effective parenting, such sessions help interest parents in further use of music at home with children and serve to bring families together at home and at church.

Church weekday programs also have opportunities to influence the musical, moral, and spiritual development of babies, ones, and twos because of the numbers of preschoolers who spend a considerable amount of time each week at day-care centers. Music helps younger preschoolers cope with the change from home to the classroom, helps them enjoy the time spent at day-care centers, and introduces them to basic spiritual concepts.

Some churches have begun informal music discovery or activity groups as a part of the preschool and children's choir schedule. These sessions are not structured in the same way choir rehearsals are for older preschoolers. Since babies, ones, and twos may already be in the church nursery when other choirs meet, why not plan some unstructured music activities for them? Use the nursery facilities for babies and the appropriate preschool rooms for ones and twos.

What Babies, Ones, and Twos Should Experience

Younger preschoolers experience music through listening, singing, and moving. Twos begin exploring music by playing classroom rhythm instruments and environmental sound sources, such as pots and pans. Through these activities, younger preschoolers are introduced to the basic building blocks of music: rhythm and melody. Children relate first to the rhythm of a song because of the words. As they mature, they begin to hear the contour of the melody.

Adults should sing to preschoolers during their early developmental stages. Younger preschoolers relate better to the rhythm and melody produced by the live, human singing voice than to any other type of instrument or recording. Children simply need to experience music at this stage of development; they do not need to label musical symbols. Fours and fives can begin to learn the name associated with the feeling of steady beat because they experienced how it felt as a two-year-old. Younger preschoolers eventually learn pitch-matching skills and the interval *sol-mi* through experiencing how *sol-mi* sounds in the context of songs sung repeatedly to them and through attempting to imitate those sounds. Set the stage for their future musical growth by providing them with an age-appropriate environment in which they *experience* music.

Selecting Appropriate Songs

Two types of songs are appropriate for use with babies, ones, and twos: (1) songs sung by adults to children and (2) spontaneous songs sung by twos based upon the songs sung by adults. Select songs to sing to babies, ones, and twos that will become a part of their song repertoire as threes, fours, and fives. Listening is a baby's first response to a song.

Most songs for children in the birth through two age group should lie within the range of middle C and second-space A in the treble clef. By selecting songs within this range to sing to them, you encourage two-year-olds to begin to match pitch. Twos tend to begin correctly matching F, E, and D within the middle C to A range more often than they match other pitches. This pitch-matching ability increases with age and singing experience.

The interval most commonly sung correctly by twos is *sol-mi*, or 5-3. Look for songs with an abundance of *sol-mi* intervals. *Stepping Stones to Matching Tones** and *Musical Experiences for Preschoolers; Birth Through Three* are good resources. Use the *sol-mi* interval to spontaneously create songs about what the children are doing. Look for songs containing *la-sol-mi* (6-5-3) and *la-sol-mi-do* (6-5-3-1). Also, look for songs that move stepwise in a descending pattern whenever possible.

Younger preschoolers enjoy singing games, nursery rhymes, and finger plays because the sounds and rhythm of the words are attractive to their ears. Songs that mention a child's name, parts of his body, or names of an animal, pet, or a family member are also good. Lullabies are excellent choices for bonding the care giver at church and at home to the child. Sing songs that are used in music activity groups for threes to younger preschoolers to familiarize them with the songs they will sing when they become threes.

Although it is important that songs selected for younger preschoolers be appropriate musically, it is even more important that the text of the songs be appropriate. Music is the medium; the text is the message—our reason for existence. See *How to Guide Preschoolers** by Jenell Strickland for appropriate and meaningful Bible thoughts for younger preschoolers. The Holman Read-to-Me Bible* also is an excellent source of appropriate Bible verses and thoughts for younger preschoolers. Study the Bible thoughts in order to understand appropriate doctrinal truths for an age group when selecting songs.

When selecting a song to use with younger preschoolers, ask the following questions:

Are the words doctrinally sound and scripturally true?

Are the words concrete?

Is the range of the melody between middle C and second-space A?

Is the song easy to sing?

Summary

Parents, Sunday School and Discipleship Training teachers, extended session workers, day-care center teachers, adult choir members, single adults, and senior adults are potential leaders of younger preschoolers in musical activities. The number of leaders needed will be determined by the number of children anticipated in a music activity group. Three adult leaders are recommended for a music activity group for babies, ones, or twos with a maximum of 12 preschoolers.

The role of leaders in musical activities for babies through twos is different from that of leaders for fours and fives, requiring active participation on an "as needed" basis. Provide a musical environment and let the children's interest and curiosity dictate the course of musical exploration and discovery.

Two types of songs are appropriate for use with babies, ones, and twos: (1) songs sung by adults to children and (2) spontaneous songs sung by twos based upon the songs sung by adults. Although selecting songs that are musically appropriate for younger preschoolers is important, it is even more important that the text of the song be appropriate.

---

*Available at Baptist Book Stores or by calling toll free 1-800-458-BSSB.

10

How Babies Through Twos Respond to Music

In order to understand the response of babies to music, leaders need to have a basic knowledge of their musical capabilities. This knowledge enables leaders to plan appropriate musical activities and to offer parents and other care givers helpful suggestions for sharing musical experiences with their children.

The Unborn Child

Listening—Listening is the first response of unborn babies to music and other sounds. They begin hearing mother's heartbeat and other environmental sounds about the third month after conception. How much babies learn through hearing these sound sources before birth has not been determined. We do know that, after the fifth month following conception, babies move in response to some sounds.

Help expectant parents in your church understand that their children's music education begins before birth. Offer parent training sessions through Discipleship Training or in special after-church fellowships to give parents ideas for listening activities for their unborn babies.

Introduce parents to songs and other types of activities which they can continue to use after their babies are born. Newborn babies recognize the parents' voices before they recognize other voices. Encourage parents to talk freely to babies, read books, read stories from the Holman Read-to-Me Bible, rhythmically chant Scripture thoughts, and sing.

Teach the parents "Jesus Loves You." Have them rock as they sing. Demonstrate how to chant the rhythm of the words. After the child is born, he will recognize the song, having heard it before his birth.

Jesus Loves You

Words by HAZEL LUCK. Music Traditional.

Encourage parents to use books from the Bible-and-Me Series* to read to their baby. The Holman Read-to-Me Bible* contains a series of 44 Bible stories written especially for preschoolers. Parents should include these stories in their family devotion times for the unborn child and his older siblings. Teaching pictures that go with the stories are included in the Read-to-Me Bible. The following excerpt is from "God Made the Birds."

"God makes birds. Birds make their nests. Birds lay eggs and sit on them. Each egg breaks open and a baby bird wiggles out. Then each baby bird learns to fly . . . God made the birds (flowers) for you and me to see."[1]

Bible thoughts are appropriate for babies through threes, and parents and care givers should rhythmically chant them to the unborn child and to children through age three.

- "I like to go to church" (Psalm 122:1).
- "Jesus went to church" (Luke 4:16).
- "We work together" (1 Corinthians 3:9).
- "We are helpers" (2 Corinthians 1:24).
- "Help one another" (Galatians 5:13).
- "Jesus loves you " (John 15:12).

- "God made the trees" (Genesis 1:11).
- "God made the stars" (Genesis 1:16).
- "God made the birds" (Genesis 1:21).
- "God made the cows" (Genesis 1:25).
- "God gives food to us" (Psalm 136:25).
- "God sends the rain" (Jeremiah 5:24).
- "God made the grass" (Genesis 1:11).
- "God is good to us" (Psalm 73:1).
- "God made the water" (Psalm 104:10).
- "God loves us" (1 John 4:10).
- "God makes the grass grow" (Psalm 104:14).
- "The moon shines in the night" (Psalm 136:9).
- "The flowers grow" (Song of Solomon 2:12).
- "God gave us ears to hear" (Proverbs 20:12).
- "God made us" (Psalm 100:3).
- "Jesus said, 'I love you' " (John 15:9).
- "Jesus said, 'You are my friends'" (John 15:14-15).
- "Jesus grew" (Luke 2:52).
- "Jesus grew tall" (Luke 2:52).
- "Jesus had friends" (Luke 2:52).
- "Jesus said, 'Love one another' " (John 15:17).

BIRTH TO ONE YEAR

From birth to one year, children grow and develop at a rapid rate. They develop musically by listening, moving in response to what they hear, and vocalizing.

Birth to Three Months

Listening—Through listening, babies from birth to three months:
- turn toward the source of a musical sound.
- are calmed by music.

Give babies many listening experiences. Parents should sing to them during daily rituals. Parents, music activity leaders, and other care givers should play appropriate recordings, provide musical crib toys, chant rhythmic Scripture thoughts, and sing comforting lullabies to them.

Parents should select songs from *Musical Experiences for Preschoolers; Birth Through Three** to use in the children's daily routines. For example, sing "God, We Thank You" and "It's Time to Eat"† during feeding times:

God, We Thank You

God, we thank You for *this day; Yes, we thank You.

God, we thank You for this day; Yes, we thank— You.

*Substitute: our food, our home, our church, our choir, our friends.

Words by MARSHA QUINN. Tune Spiritual. Words © copyright 1974 Broadman Press (SESAC). All rights reserved. International copyright secured.

Sing "I Am Very Special" when changing diapers or bathing babies.

I Am Very Special

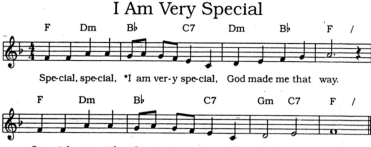

Spe-cial, spe-cial, *I am ver-y spe-cial, God made me that way.

Spe-cial, spe-cial, I am ver-y spe-cial, God made me!

*Substitute: you are . . . God made you that way.

Words and music by DERRELL BILLINGSLEY. © Copyright 1977 Broadman Press (SESAC). All rights reserved. International copyright secured.

Babies respond better to a person singing than to a recording. However, recordings of instrumental music featuring high-pitched instruments, such as flutes and violins, are interesting to babies. Babies enjoy music from the Baroque and Classical periods of music history. Select recordings, such as Tchaikovsky's *The Nutcracker,* Bach's *Brandenburg Concer-*

tos, and Mozart's *Eine kleine Nachtmusik.* Play recordings often for babies in the nursery.

Crib music box toys encourage babies to listen. Attach the music boxes to cribs and play them often.

Lullabies are important listening and bonding activities between babies and care givers. Select lullabies from *Musical Experiences for Preschoolers; Birth Through Three.** Sing these songs often to calm babies. "Jesus Loves You" is an excellent song for laying a proper spiritual and musical foundation for babies.

Rhythmic chanting also encourages babies to listen and turn toward the source of the sound. Babies are fascinated by the rhythm of speech.

Moving—Babies from birth to three months move in response to musical sounds they hear. This movement is vital to future language skills and muscle development. Encourage them to move by singing and talking to them and playing recordings and musical instruments for them.

Vocalizing—Babies from birth to three months express feelings by crying. Before they begin making babbling sounds, they use their voices to cry. Crying is a form of communication with care givers and is an important step in learning to express feelings through making vocal sounds.

Three to Six Months

Listening—Through listening, babies from three to six months:
- continue to turn toward the source of musical sound.
- continue to be calmed by music, especially lullabies.

Continue to use the same songs and recordings in daily routines and in the nursery that you used with unborn children and babies from birth to three months. Expand the use of musical crib toys to include those that are red and yellow to attract babies' attention. Make sure musical crib toys make accurate musical pitches rather than approximate pitches. Continue to rhythmically chant Scripture thoughts. Lullabies still have a calming effect on babies.

Use finger plays and action songs to interest babies in music.

Sing "Here Is the Beehive,"† "I'm a Little Teapot,"† "Open, Shut Them,"† and "Where Is Thumbkin?"† to babies. The motions, in addition to the music, hold babies' attention and encourage their movement and babbling.

Sing "Riding in My Car" when traveling with the family in the car.

Riding in My Car

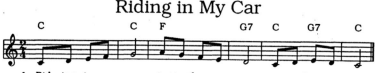

1. Rid - ing in my car, sing-ing hap-py songs, sing-ing hap-py songs.
2. Work-ing in the yard, help-ing Dad-dy mow, help-ing Dad-dy mow.

From "Sentence Songs." Words and music by AL WASHBURN. © Copyright 1976 Broadman Press (SESAC). All rights reserved. International copyright secured.

Moving—Babies from three to six months continue moving in response to sounds they hear. Sometime during the three to six months they stop moving and turn toward the source of the music. The sound of music boxes and metronomes often causes babies to stop and listen to musical sounds. Use a variety of environmental and musical sounds to attract their attention. Give the babies rubber manipulative toys with bells inside. The musical sound will encourage their movement. Install musical mobiles over the crib. Babies will try to stretch their arms toward the musical sound by age five or six months. Put wind chimes in the nursery. Play a variety of musical instruments for babies from ages three to six months and watch their responses. Play a variety of active recordings, such as J. S. Bach's *Brandenburg Concertos,* to aid in motor skill development.

Vocalizing—Babies from three to six months vocalize by:
• crying to express feelings.
• making babbling sounds.

Encourage babies' babbling sounds by smiling at them whenever they babble. Notice which songs, recordings, and musical activities elicit the most babbling sounds, and repeat those activities often. Read stories from the Bible-and-Me Series and from the Holman Read-to-Me Bible so babies can hear the rhythm of the words.

Six to Twelve Months

Listening—From six to nine months, babies develop listening skills by:
- turning toward the source of the musical sound.
- discovering that music is more than lullabies.
- beginning to listen intently.

From nine to twelve months, babies refine their listening skills by showing musical preferences.·

Continue to use familiar songs in daily routines while feeding, rocking, bathing, diapering, and dressing babies. Although lullabies are the most important songs for babies from birth to six months, babies from six to nine months discover that other songs are interesting. They listen intently to an adult or sibling singing. They enjoy live performances or recordings of instruments. They stare at stereo speakers and performers. Smiles appear on their faces when they hear music boxes, and they often attempt to reach for the sound. Sing songs in which the names of the baby, family members, and pets can be inserted (since babies are beginning to learn these names). Songs, such as "I Am Happy,"† "Jesus Loves Joe,"† "Thank You, God, for Daddy,"† "I Love My Mother,"† "Everybody Loves Baby,"† "Jesus Loves You,"† and "What Can Billy Do?"† help reinforce hearing babies' names and interest them in listening to the song. Sing "I Feed My Kitty" and insert the name of the family cat in the song.

I Feed My Kitty

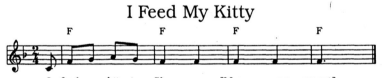

I feed my kit-ty. She says, "Meow, meow, meow."

Between nine and twelve months of age, babies begin to show that they like or dislike music they hear. They turn away from certain sound sources, look unhappy, and sometimes cry. Give babies a variety of musical experiences so they can develop preferences for music. Remember that most preferences are shaped by the home musical environment. If a variety of musical styles is presented in children's musical experiences before they are born and up to nine months of age, they will prefer a broader spectrum of music.

Moving—From six to nine months, babies begin to sway and move up and down after listening intently to music. By giving babies a variety of listening experiences before they are six months old, their moving responses will happen sooner than if they were not in a musical environment. Begin organized moving activities with swaying and moving up and down, for these movements are natural to children. Babies from six to twelve months enjoy water play. Provide plastic floating animals and fish and sing songs about the toys to babies. Watch their interest in playing with the toys and listen to their babbling as they play. Bouncing babies on your knees and clapping your hands onto babies' outstretched palms encourages them to continue bouncing or to attempt to clap your hands when you stop the activity. Bounce or clap while listening to "Sittin' in a High Chair" from Hap Palmer's *Babysong* (Educational Activities, Inc. recording).

Walk while holding babies. Bounce or stroke them to the steady beat of a recording or song. The obvious steady beat and the quick tempos make the *Hooked on Classics* series of recordings an excellent resource for this type of activity.

From nine to twelve months, babies remember simple motions to nursery songs, simple finger plays, and action songs. Teach appropriate nursery songs, finger plays, and action songs to parents and other care givers to use at home. Repetition is important in younger preschoolers' learning. Use puppets and other visual aids to attract babies' attention. Make a bright yellow felt multipurpose glove, and attach Velcro to each finger and the thumb of the glove.

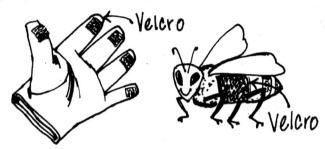

Purchase five small chenille bees, monkeys, ducks, pigs, (and other insects, birds, or animals commonly mentioned in children's songs) from a craft store. Glue a small piece of Velcro to each bee. Attach one bee on each finger and the thumb of the glove. Sing "Here Is the Beehive" to babies, using the glove to let the bees out of the hive.

Here Is the Beehive

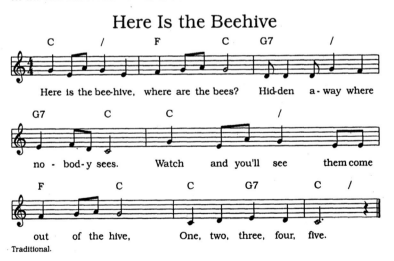

Traditional.

Replace the bees on the glove with other insects, birds, or animals when singing other finger plays. Similar gloves can be purchased from early childhood education suppliers, but homemade gloves are less expensive.

Encourage babies to move their legs by sewing jingle bells in baby socks.

Turn down the top of the sock and securely sew three or four jingle bells purchased from a craft shop under the turned-down sock top. Sew the turned down sock top to the sock, making a casing for the jingle bells.

Vocalizing—From six to nine months, babies attempt to make vocal sounds:
- that are different from melodies and rhythms heard.
- before they attempt to speak.

Babies sometimes make musical, babbling sounds after moving in response to music they enjoy. They cannot match words, rhythm, or pitch, but they attempt to babble musically.

From nine to twelve months, babies:
- attempt to sing short songs.
- begin to imitate the words of a song.

Babies try to imitate sounds and fragments of familiar songs. Repetitive texts and tunes, songs in which children's names can be inserted, and songs with familiar environmental sounds are important. Babies enjoy finger plays and action songs and try to imitate simple motions.

Encourage babies to vocalize by repeating simple songs frequently as a part of daily routines. Read books and sing related songs. Rhythmically chant and sing Scripture thoughts. Sing to babies while watching them play. Make music an important part of babies' environments.

Exploring Environmental Sound Sources—Allow babies to

experiment with old cooking utensils, pots, pans, and empty plastic containers. Demonstrate the different sounds kitchen items make when beaten or scraped. Make musical kick toys by placing jingle bells inside of crib bumper pads to encourage babies to kick or hit the bumper pad to hear the bell sound. Babies also enjoy balls with jingle bells inside. Musical push and pull toys encourage babies to move them to hear the sounds they make.

Ones

Listening—Ones begin to listen to music without being distracted. They want to listen to music without interruption, and their listening attention span is longer than those from birth to one year. They show an obvious preference for certain songs, recordings, and styles of music. They want frequent repetition of favorite recordings and sometimes bring those recordings to adults to play.

Provide a musical environment for ones, assuring them of many listening experiences. Singing to ones at every opportunity motivates their interest in music. Hearing a variety of recordings and musical instruments introduces ones to a variety of different sounds. Sing name recognition songs to children "Jesus Loves Joe"† and "Jesus Loves You" are good songs to attract children's interest. Sing "A Helper,"† "I Can Help,"† and "God, We Thank You" during daily routines. Ones also enjoy hearing adults sing rhymes to them.

Moving—After listening, ones respond to music by moving. From twelve to eighteen months, ones experience:
- large movements to music.
- varying movements to music.
- use of space when moving.
- repetition of some movements.

Although twelve- to eighteen-month-olds move in response to music they hear, their movements are not coordinated with the music.

From eighteen to twenty-four months, ones respond by:
- moving to music with other persons.
- moving while attempting to sing.

• attempting unsuccessfully to coordinate their movements to the rhythm of the music.

Watch ones as they respond to music by crawling or toddling to the sound source. They stare with great delight and interest at stereo speakers, music boxes, metronomes, singers, and musical instruments they hear. They make large, obvious movements to music and move to music for longer periods of time than when they were babies. Ones enjoy bouncing to music they hear, and they like to move about with favorite toys or adults when hearing music. Many ones sway, bounce, bend their knees, and jump while listening to music.

Encourage ones to move to music by moving with them when they listen to recordings or to you sing. Sing "Can You Clap Your Hands?" and other action songs to inspire ones to move as you sing.

Can You Clap Your Hands?

Can you clap your hands?   I   can,   I   can;

Can you clap your hands?   I   can clap my hands.

Push toys with jingle bells or other musical sounds prompt ones to move when they hear the musical sounds. Ones also enjoy rocking while parents and other care givers sing to them.

Ones enjoy water play. Playing in the water with plastic dolls, floating ducks, and turtles with bells inside help children develop their small muscles. Play recordings and sing for ones while they are bathing or while they are playing with water. Provide manipulatives for small-muscle development. Since ones enjoy emptying trash cans and other objects, sing about what they are doing when you observe them emptying containers. Sing "What Can Billy Do?" at such a time.

Provide as many opportunities as possible for ones to develop large and small muscles. Objects that will help in this development are puzzles, manipulatives, blocks, balls, books, classroom rhythm instruments, and musical toys. Use songs and other musical activities while the children play.

Vocalizing—Ones from twelve to eighteen months:
- attempt to sing short songs.
- begin to imitate the words of a song.

Ones at this developmental stage like to listen to the rhythm of the words of rhymes. They enjoy the sound of the music. They try to respond by singing, but it is still a musical babbling sound. It is not unusual to see ones vocalizing by themselves. By eighteen months of age, ones' babblings begin to sound like singing. Their favorite songs are rhymes and songs with animal sounds. They enjoy humming while playing. "I Feed My Kitty," † and "God Cares for You" † are good repetitive songs that ones will attempt to imitate.

Ones from eighteen to twenty-four months:
- continue to imitate the words of a song.
- sing spontaneously in everyday activities.
- imitate rhythms and melodies of songs.
- model their singing after adults' singing.

Some ones at this developmental stage attempt to vocalize while moving and others sing while sitting. By about nineteen months of age, parents and other care givers begin hearing ones sing actual pitches that sound like adults' pitches because they are trying to imitate adults' singing. The intervals most commonly sung by ones are the major second and major and minor thirds.

Major second

Major third

Minor third

When children reach this stage of vocal development, they are often heard singing while they play and conduct their everyday routines. Many ones sing to themselves when waking in the morning or from a nap or just before going to sleep.

Ones also like to sing songs in which their names or the

names of family members and pets can be inserted. Since they are learning to point to parts of their bodies named by an adult, sing "Clap Your Hands" to give them the opportunity to listen to the music while identifying different parts of their bodies.

Clap Your Hands

1. Clap your hands, tap your fin-gers, Touch your nose, pull your ear;
2. Stand up tall, snap your fin-gers, Touch your toes, pull your hair;

Nod your head, pat your foot, Ev - 'ry - bod - y sing.
Shake your head, sit right down, Ev - 'ry - bod - y sing.

Sing echo songs, songs with repeated texts and tunes, and songs with animal sounds. These comprise the most success- ful singing attempts of ones. Ones spend much of their time imitating the actions of adults. Use singing conversation often, and use children's names in the singing conversation. Sing within their limited range, between middle C and second- space A, since most of the pitches ones match center around E.

How are you to-day, Jim?

I am glad to see you.

Use these pitches often in singing to ones. All children even- tually sing these intervals while playing.

Sing "What Can Billy Do?" as often as possible, inserting children's names in the song for Billy's name and substituting activities of ones for those of Billy.

Sing "I Feed My Kitty"† and insert the name of the family cat in the song while feeding the cat. Ask the children to make the "meow" sound of the kitty. The sound helps them discover the high sounds their voices can make. This discovery helps them

What Can Billy Do?

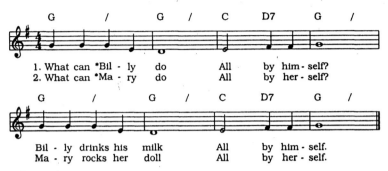

1. What can *Bil - ly do   All   by him - self?
2. What can *Ma - ry do   All   by her - self?

Bil - ly drinks his   milk   All   by him - self.
Ma - ry rocks her   doll   All   by her - self.

*Substitute other names.

Words by ALMA MAY SCARBOROUGH. Music by TERRY KIRKLAND. From *Living with Preschoolers,*
October-December 1973. © Copyright 1973 The Sunday School Board of the Southern Baptist
Convention. All rights reserved.

find their singing voices and later expand their singing ranges.

Sing "Jesus Loves You,"† substituting the names of ones for
"you" in the song. Show ones how to rock their favorite toys
while you sing the song, inserting the name of a favorite toy for
"you."

Help ones develop a positive self-image by singing "I Am Very
Special"† to them, substituting their names for "I" and "you"
in the song. Sing the song to foster good behavior, being helpers, and good eating habits.

Sing spontaneously about what children are doing as they
play. "Stack the Blocks"† is a good song related to play activities.

Stack the Blocks

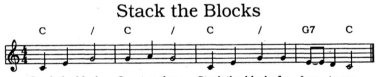

Stack the blocks, One, two,three; Stack the blocks for *me_ to see.

*Substitute: Mommy, Daddy, teacher, etc.

Words and music by VETERIA (TEE) BILLINGSLEY. From *Easy Songs for Early Singers.* © Copyright
1985 Van Ness Press, Inc. (ASCAP). All rights reserved. International copyright secured.

Sing the song to attract ones' attention. Continue with singing conversations about each child's work.

Jay   built a bridge.   Beck- y made a house with blocks.

"A Helper,"† "I Can Help,"† " I Will Be a Helper,"† "Roll the Ball,"† and "What Can Billy Do?"† are appropriate songs to use with activities for ones. Keep in mind that ones, on first hearing a song, concentrate more on the words and rhythm of the words than on the melody. Although texts are extremely important in fostering spiritual development, children also need to hear some melodies without texts to help them develop musically. Introduce ones to melodies without words by humming, giving them the opportunity to concentrate on the music.

Vary the tempos, dynamics, and types of melodies that you sing without words so ones can experience a variety of musical sounds. Occasionally, demonstrate varying movements to the songs without words so the children will imitate you.

Twos

Twos experience music through listening, moving, singing, and exploring sound sources. They are able to enjoy more types of musical activities than ones.

Listening—Twos, through listening:

• continue to listen to music for longer periods of time than ones.

• become aware of the rhythm of the words of a song, fast and slow, and loud and soft.

• recognize a song by the sound of the words.

Since twos enjoy listening to music actively, sing to them at every opportunity, especially during daily routines. Most twos are ritualistic and expect routines to be the same each time. Music can be an enjoyable part of these routines. For blessings at mealtimes, sing "God, We Thank You,"† "Thank You, Dear

God,"† "Thank You, God,"† or "Thank You, God, for Every-thing."† Sing "It's Time to Eat"† to signal meal times.

It's Time to Eat

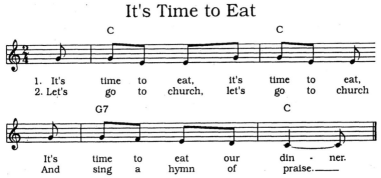

From "Sentence Songs." Words and music by AL WASHBURN. © Copyright 1976 Broadman Press (SESAC). All rights reserved. International copyright secured.

Twos listen to and learn the songs you sing to them. They also try to sing them, usually devising their own songs based upon those songs they have heard. Keep a portable cassette recorder within reach to record twos when you hear them singing. Then, let them hear themselves on the recording.

Provide a variety of listening experiences for twos. The following recordings are appropriate: *Hymns for Quiet Times,** *More Hymns for Quiet Times,** *Music for Quiet Times,** the last movement of Mozart's *Sonata No. 11 in A major* (K. 331), *Hooked on Classics* series,[2] and Benjamin Britten's *Young Person's Guide to the Orchestra.*[2]

Select recordings that feature an assortment of instrumental sounds, different tempos, and changing dynamics so twos will learn to appreciate and understand a variety of music styles. These sounds enable twos to develop muscle skills when they move in response to what they hear.

Twos learn about life by watching and imitating adults. Use every opportunity to sing spontaneously to twos, describing their activities. Because they are interested in imitating adults, they will enjoy listening to and eventually trying to sing adults' songs. Sing "God Helps Me"† when twos help with household chores, "I Feed My Kitty"† when they help feed family pets, "A Helper"† whenever they help with chores at home or at church.

A Helper

Oh, I will be a help - er and do what I can!

Use the universal childhood chant *(sol-mi-la-sol-mi)* to devise your own songs to interest twos in listening.

God made the wa - ter.   God gave us ears to hear.

Play musical instruments often. Twos enjoy seeing and hearing the sound source, and will begin experiencing, visually and aurally, how melodies move. Hearing instruments played also encourages twos to try to sing.

Use opportunities, like traveling in the family car, to listen to recordings and sing songs with twos. Sometimes they do not enjoy traveling, but they do enjoy music activities and the attention they receive from adults and siblings.

Moving—Twos move in response to what they have hear when listening to a recording, a musical instrument, or a song. They respond by:

- moving less to music than when they were babies.
- moving after hearing many repetitions of a song or recording.
- continuing unsuccessfully in their attempts to coordinate movements to the rhythm of the music.

Twos move less when hearing music than when they were babies because they are beginning to concentrate on listening to the movement of the melody. After they hear many repetitions of a song or recording, they move in response to what they hear. Choose songs with repeated rhythmic, melodic, and textual patterns so twos will have the opportunity to listen and respond by moving to what they hear. The repetition in songs speeds the time twos need to remember what they have heard and to move in response. Provide scarves, brightly-colored ribbons, crepe paper streamers taped to the end of empty cardboard paper towel rolls, and other materials to encourage twos to move. Let children select an object and ask them to swing their object in the air as they listen to the recordings. Help them to run and tiptoe on the fast parts of the music and to walk and slide their feet slowly on the slow parts of the music, swinging the objects as they move. Demonstrate some movements for twos without insisting that they use the same movements. Show them you are pleased by singing songs, such as "You're a Special Child"† and by smiling and participating with them in moving.

Vocalizing—After listening to and moving in response to music, twos try to sing and recreate what they have heard. They respond vocally by:

- continuing to sing spontaneously.
- enjoying singing alone, not in groups.
- singing longer songs and singing them more often than when they were babies.
- learning songs by chanting words and rhythms (by age two-and-one-half).

Select songs that lie in the range of middle C to second-space A to teach to two-year-olds. Many twos begin matching adults' melodies around E, F, and F♯ above middle C. They may chant some parts of a song and sing some parts. Some twos sing entire short, repetitive songs because this music has been a part of their environments from conception. All twos enjoy songs in which the names of family, pets, and their names can be inserted. They also enjoy songs that contain animal sounds they can imitate. Sing "I Feed My Kitty"† with twos. After they are familiar with the song, cut a large cat-head pattern from heavy cardboard. Then, cut a large mouth in the head and glue fake fur on the cat head, leaving the mouth opening uncovered. Glue felt eyes, ears, nose, and a mouth on the cat. Make the mouth opening large so that twos can put their hands through the opening. Attach a round piece of cardboard, such as an empty paper towel roll, to the back of the cat to serve as a handle. Put a red sock on your hand and arm and put them through the cat's mouth from the back, similar to a cat's tongue. Cut large paper circles from brightly colored construction paper. Let twos "feed" the paper circles into the cardboard cat head's tongue in the large mouth while you sing "I Feed My Kitty."† Encourage twos to make the "meow" sound while feeding the cat.

Make patterns of dogs, ducks, and other animals, and substitute their names and vocal sounds for those of the cat in "I Feed My Kitty."†

Provide opportunities for twos to hear unaccompanied singing. Select songs that can be used on many occasions so twos will hear them repeated often and will be encouraged to try to sing them. Sing songs, such as "You're a Special Child,"† when twos are eating, bathing, toileting, or dressing. When you have given verbal approval of their accomplishments, singing songs affirms and helps build their self-esteem. Sing "A Helper"† whenever twos try to help with household chores. Sing "Jesus Loves You"† at bedtime and when comforting or rocking twos.

Select songs with repetitive animal sounds to sing with twos. Sing "Six Little Ducks"† and ask twos to imitate the animal sounds. Making train whistle sounds when singing "Engine, Engine, Number Nine"† and wind sounds when singing "If I Were the Wind"† to twos helps them learn to find their singing voices.

Twos like to sing spontaneously. Introduce songs while reading to them. Use stories from the Read-to-Me Bible and from the Bible-and-Me Series along with appropriate songs selected from *Musical Experiences for Preschoolers; Birth Through Three.* Give twos access to the books used with the songs to encourage them to look at the books when they are playing and to sing spontaneously. Listen to see if they imitate parts, repetitive words, or animal sounds in the songs you have sung. If you cannot find appropriate songs for the stories you have chosen, create your own songs, using the childhood chant (*sol-mi-la-sol-mi*).

Make singing a part of family devotion times. Sing blessings at mealtimes. Simple hymn fragments, such as the refrains of "There Is a Name I Love to Hear" (No. 66, *BH*, 1975) and "O Come, All Ye Faithful" (No. 81, *BH*, 1975) also can be introduced to twos since they possibly will be sung in music activity times for fours and fives. Learning these hymns later, when they become fours and fives, will be easier, having heard them as twos and threes. Allow twos to participate as they wish in the short devotion times. They do not enjoy group singing opportunities as much as they enjoy individual singing, and they do not match pitch well when they sing in groups. Encourage their singing attempts but do not force them to sing with the entire family.

Remember that twos will sing longer songs and will sing those songs more often than they did as babies. They can be heard vocalizing from the time they awake in the morning until they go to sleep at night. Reinforce this newfound enthusiasm for singing by singing together in home and family activities.

Provide many opportunities for twos to sing at church, remembering that the most effective singing times for twos are when they are singing alone. Plan to use singing as a part of learning centers that are already provided in twos' educational rooms. Use the homeliving center to encourage twos to sing spontaneously as they imitate adults' actions. Participate with twos as they play in the homeliving center and be prepared to create your own songs, using pitches of the childhood chant as you watch the children playing. Listen to twos as they create their own songs or respond to songs you sing to them. Many of them will stop their activities in the homeliving center and listen when you sing "It's Fun to Work,"† "A Helper,"† "God, We Thank You,"† or "It's Time to Eat."†

Provide puzzles for twos. The puzzles should consist of two or three pieces with brightly colored, simple pictures. Using the childhood chant, sing spontaneously created songs about what you see in the puzzles or about the children working the puzzles. Sing "God Helps Me,"† substituting "I can work a puzzle" for "I can rake the leaves that fall" in the song. Sing "I Feed My Kitty"† when twos work a puzzle of a cat picture. Make your own puzzles for twos to fit songs you want to sing to them or to fit songs they are learning at home and in church organizations. Glue pictures from coloring books to heavy cardboard and laminate or cover them with clear, adhesive-backed plastic. Cut a laminated picture into two or three pieces and put it in the puzzle area with other puzzles. Sing songs related to the new puzzle.

Make music an integral part of the block area for twos. Allow them to listen to recordings while they work. Sing "God Helps Me"† and "Stack the Blocks"† unaccompanied while you watch them work. Compose spontaneous songs related to their block activities. Sing "What Can Billy Do?"† so the children can insert their own names in the song. Provide wooden play toys and help twos create their own role-playing scenes. Then, sing about those scenes.

Make books an important learning center for twos at church. Include a variety of books with bright pictures of twos in everyday activities. Several book series are available for twos at Baptist Book Stores: Bible-and-Me Series for twos and threes; Gibson Plastic Books; Good Little Books; Child Experiences Books; My Shape Books; Please Read-to-Me Series; and God Made Series. Consider singing some of the stories, using pitches of the childhood chant instead of merely reading them. Observe twos as they try to sing while turning the pages of the books and looking at the pictures. They will talk and sing to themselves while looking at the books.

A manipulative center aids in muscle development of twos and encourages singing while they play. Include large beads to string, varying size balls, pegboards, plastic nesting cups, and items with lids. Twos enjoy singing to themselves while playing in the manipulative center, and they enjoy hearing adults respond to them by singing. Sing about what you observe them doing with manipulatives:

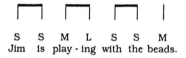

S   S   M   L   S   S   M
Jim is play - ing with the beads.

Select other songs that describe what they are doing, such as "Roll the Ball."† Listen for twos' singing attempts and try to determine if the songs they sing sound similar to other songs they know.

Twos enjoy the role-playing center as much as or more than any other learning center. Provide twos with used adult clothing and jewelry items. Allow them to dress in these items and role-play adult actions. Twos will abruptly travel from learning center to learning center and many times will leave the role-playing area wearing some of the clothing or jewelry items. Sometimes they choose to go to the homeliving center where they will role-play home life. Listen as they sing familiar lullabies like "Jesus Loves You" † to baby dolls in the homeliving center while still wearing some of the adult clothing items. They will attempt to compose their own songs as they role-play.

Observe twos playing in the large-muscle area with push and pull toys, in the tunnels, in tents, and on the rocking horse. Sing "God Helps Me" † and "What Can Billy Do?" † as you observe the children playing. Listen for their singing attempts as they push, pull, rock, and crawl in the large-muscle area. Be prepared to create your own spontaneous songs about their activities.

Provide a nature center periodically to allow twos to explore things that God has created. Include varying types of plants, leaves, seashells, rocks, pet fish, pet hamsters or gerbils, and other small nature items. Instead of simply talking about the items in the nature center, sing about the items. Answer twos' questions with singing conversation.

Plan many small-group and individual singing activities in addition to the learning center activities. Twos enjoy water play. Have plastic squirt bottles available with a little water in them, washable paints in old plastic butter containers, and plastic floating toys. Twos like to sing while they play with the water items. Leaders can sing songs, such as "What Can Billy Do?," † while watching twos play. Children can do water-play activities alongside each other (parallel play) or alone. Parallel play is good, but it still will not entice twos to sing in groups. They do not enjoy group activities as much as individual activities. Twos like playing in large boxes or playing in a sandbox, and they sing often when engaged in these activities.

Include singing games, nursery rhymes, and finger plays in songs you sing to twos. Singing games, such as "Can You Clap Your Hands?,"† and finger plays, such as "Here Is the Beehive,"† encourage twos to move initially. Later, they will sing in response to the movements they make.

Use puppets frequently with twos. Twos will sometimes sing for a puppet when they will not sing for an adult. Washable oven mitts, shaped like cats, frogs, lambs, horses, zebras, and other animals, are available from kitchen specialty shops and linen outlet stores. Several puppet manufacturers make realistic animal hand puppets. Use an animal puppet to illustrate a song after twos have heard a song about that animal repeated many times. Use the animal puppets to encourage the children to make a sound similar to that of an animal.

At two-and-a-half years of age, children learn songs by chanting the words, and they learn the rhythm before learning the melody. Rhythmically chant the Bible thoughts appropriate for ages birth through three on pages 78-79. After many repetitions of the chant, add the pitches of the childhood chant to create the melody of the song.

Use these chants at home in family devotion times and other activities. They also can be used in a variety of church activities.

Playing Instruments—After listening, moving, and vocalizing, twos want to create their own music by exploring environmental sound sources and playing instruments. Body instruments are the most obvious instruments that twos can play. Sing "Can You Clap Your Hands?"† and guide the children to discover the different types of sounds their body instruments can make. One of the most natural movements for twos is *patschen* (patting the thighs).

Provide a music focus area for twos in the learning center. Include rhythm sticks, step bells, wrist bells, maracas, sand blocks, woodblocks, tone blocks, cluster bells, triangles, hand cymbals, finger cymbals, tambourines, Indian tom-tom drums, hand drums, and other rhythm instruments. Avoid using jingle taps and other dangerous instruments that have large nails protruding from them. These could seriously injure the children. Introduce a few types of instruments each week. Group similar types of instruments to be presented: rhythm sticks, woodblocks, and tone blocks; step bells, wrist bells, cluster bells, triangles, hand cymbals, and finger cymbals; and tambourines, Indian tom-tom drums, and hand drums. Since twos do not understand the concept of sharing, provide plenty of instruments so the children will not try to take instruments away from each other.

Provide other types of experiences for twos, such as experimenting with plastic bowls, large plastic utensils, pots and pans, lids, wire whisks, and other unbreakable kitchen items. Encourage them to listen to the different types of sounds these items can make.

Try to coordinate teaching efforts between home and church in teaching songs so twos hear some of the same songs at home and at church.

Summary

Listening is the unborn child's first response to music and other sounds. He begins hearing his mother's heartbeat and other environmental sounds about the third month after conception. Help expectant parents in your church understand that a child's music education begins before birth. Introduce parents to songs and other types of activities which they can continue to use after their child is born.

Give babies many listening experiences. Sing to them during daily rituals. Play appropriate recordings in the nursery. Provide musical crib toys, chant rhythmic Bible thoughts, and sing comforting lullabies to them.

From birth to one year, children grow and develop at a rapid rate. They develop musically by listening, moving in response to what they hear, and vocalizing. Ones begin to listen to music without being distracted. They want to listen without interruption, and their listening attention spans are longer than those from birth to one year.

After listening, ones respond to music by moving. From 12 to 18 months, ones experience large movements to music, varying movements to music, use of space when moving, and repetition of some movements. From 18 to 24 months, ones respond by moving to music with other people, moving while attempting to sing, and attempting unsuccessfully to coordinate their movements to the rhythm of the music.

Ones from 18 to 24 months continue to imitate the words of a song, sing spontaneously in everyday activities, imitate rhythms and melodies of songs, and model their singing after adults' singing. Sing echo songs, songs with repeated texts and tunes, and songs with animal sounds to ones.

Twos, through listening continue to listen to music for longer periods of time than ones, become aware of the rhythm of the words of a song, fast and slow, and loud and soft, and recognize a song by the sound of the words. Twos listen to and learn the songs you sing to them. They also try to sing them, usually devising their own songs based upon those songs they have heard.

Twos move in response to what they have heard when listening to a recording, a musical instrument, or a song. They respond by moving less to music than when they were babies, moving after hearing many repetitions of a song or recording, and continuing unsuccessfully in their attempts to coordinate movements to the rhythm of the music.

After listening to and moving in response to music, twos try to sing and recreate what they have heard. They respond vocally by continuing to sing spontaneously; enjoying singing alone (not in groups), singing longer songs and singing them more often than when they were babies; and learning songs by chanting words and rhythms (by age two-and-one-half).

Provide opportunities for twos to hear unaccompanied singing. Select songs with repetitive animal sounds. Twos like to sing spontaneously. Remember that twos will sing longer songs and will sing those songs more often than they did as babies. Provide many opportunities for twos to sing at church, remembering that the most effective singing times for twos are when they are singing alone. Plan to use singing as a part of learning centers that are already provided in twos' educational rooms.

After listening, moving, and vocalizing, twos want to create their own music by exploring environmental sound sources and playing instruments. Body instruments are the most obvious instruments that twos can play.

Coordinate teaching efforts between home and church in teaching songs so twos hear some of the same songs at home and at church.

1"God Made the Birds," Read-to-Me Bible, p. 20b. © Copyright 1984 Holman Bible Publishers. All rights reserved. Used by permission.

2Available from Educational Record Center, Building 400/Suite 400, 1575 Northside Drive, Northwest, Atlanta, Georgia 30318.

*Available at Baptist Book Stores.

†Songs from Musical Experiences for Preschoolers; Birth Through Three.

11

Leading Musical Activities
for Babies Through Twos

Expectations

Providing an appropriate musical environment at church for babies, ones, and twos will lead them to love music and enjoy coming to church. These early musical experiences will make music their lifetime friend and provide a means for self-expression. By the time they are four and five years old, they will be prepared to begin acquiring the skills necessary for developing musical concepts that will ultimately lead to membership in a performing choir as an elementary-age child.

Babies, ones, and twos should not be expected to perform during fellowship times or share during worship services at church. The purpose of musical activities for younger preschoolers is to provide opportunities for musical and spiritual growth and development of the children. Expect babies, ones, and twos to be inquisitive about the musical environment provided at church. Allow them to freely explore that environment. Some twos prefer working alone to working in groups. Plan activities with those children in mind. Music leaders for younger preschoolers are not as visible to the congregation as other choir directors. However, the work these loving leaders do to provide musical and spiritual training is vitally important to the musical development and spiritual growth of the children.

Continuing to study the developmental characteristics of younger preschoolers is important. One of the frightening current problems in our society is the pushing of preschoolers to do too much, too soon. Dr. David Elkind, a noted child psychologist, thinks that adults feel pressured to make children learn to do tasks, such as reading and arithmetic, at very early ages so they will be ahead of other children in school. The results of this pressure, what he calls "calendar hurrying," are frustration and low self-images in the children.[1] As leaders of babies, ones, and twos in the church, we must be careful not to frustrate the children by planning activities that are beyond their understanding and ability.

Decisions

In choosing activities for babies, ones, and twos, consider the number of children involved. Obviously, a movement activity with 25 two-year-olds in a small room will be difficult. The more children involved in a music activity group, the more individual and small-group activities are needed. Supply learning centers with play items. Play recordings and sing songs near these areas.

The available facilities will influence the types of activities you choose. If it is necessary to be in a room other than a preschool room, bring blocks and other items to the room each week to create block centers, nature centers, and homeliving centers. The shape of the room also influences the decision about activities to select. Group quiet play activities in one part of the room and louder activities in another part of the room.

The decision to involve parents or not will also determine the type of activities you select. One or two leaders can successfully lead parents and their children in musical activities in a parent-involvement approach. The leaders set up the activities and serve as guides. Without parents, more leaders are needed to participate with the children. In either case, parents should be encouraged to participate in musical activities at home with their babies, ones, and twos by singing to them and playing a variety of recordings for them. Give the parents ideas of activities to share at home with their children. Encourage parents to use activities from *Musical Experiences for Preschoolers; Birth Through Three.** Model these activities for them during the music activity time at church.

Pacing

Babies, ones, and twos have short attention spans. When preschoolers tire of an activity, they are finished with that activity—even if the leader is not. Be sensitive to the needs of the children. If they appear to be frustrated by an activity, move on to another activity. That particular activity is probably too difficult or uninteresting to the children that day.

Babies, ones, and twos like repetition. Too many new songs or activities introduced in one music activity time frustrates the children. Plan to use a song in a variety of ways over a period of several weeks. After hearing songs many times, children respond to them by moving and, eventually, by babbling or trying to sing key words. The key to pacing is having a good lesson plan with other ideas ready for use if needed.

Management

A popular misconception of a music activity group is one in which children sit quietly in a circle and sing cute songs. Sitting quietly for an extended period of time is impossible for the age group. Visual aids are necessary to attract the attention of younger preschoolers and to effectively engage them in an activity. Vary the activities to include listening, moving, singing, and experimenting with sounds. Large-group time should be introduced to twos and used for limited singing experiences and moving activities. Include movement activities each week. Younger preschoolers enjoy moving and must experience different responses to music before they can learn the terms for them. Use of puppets, scarves, ribbons, whispered instructions, and conversational singing in transition between activities will keep the children interested in participating. The degree of learning is not necessarily related to the degree in which the children participate in activities. Many twos will quietly watch a leader sing, then go home after the music activity time and attempt to sing the songs they heard at church. Have plenty of supplies available for the children to use in the learning centers. Twos do not enjoy sharing and do not understand why they have to give up an instrument or musical toy to another child. Maintaining an interesting pace in the music activity time also will help the leaders keep the children involved in the activities.

An extremely *quiet* preschool room is not a *happy* preschool room. Younger preschoolers who feel free to use their speaking voices and to make up songs as they play in learning centers will enjoy coming to church and will learn more than children who are asked to be quiet.

Summary

Music should be a part of the environment for babies, ones, and twos. Their environment includes the home, the church nursery, Sunday School, Discipleship Training, the day-care center, and informal music discovery or activity times as a part of the Music Ministry choir schedule. Babies, ones, and twos should experience music through listening, singing, and movement. The music activity groups at church are not intended to be organized performing choirs but opportunities for musical and spiritual growth and development for the children. Sing songs about the child's daily routines, God, and Jesus. Prayer songs, singing games, nursery rhymes, and finger plays are effective types of songs to use with younger preschoolers. Plan flexible activities according to the developmental characteristics of babies, ones, and twos.

Resources

Core List of Songs
A Helper†
Baby Jesus in the Manger†
Bye, Baby Bunting†
Church Time††
Can You Clap Your Hands?†
Creeping, Crawling†
Doggy, Doggy†
Engine, Engine, Number Nine†
Everybody Loves Baby†
Fall Leaves††
Farm Animals††
Farm Friends††
God Cares for You†
God Loves Me††
God Helps Me†
God Made Everyone†

God Makes the Wind Blow†
God, We Thank You†
God's World Is a Wonderful Place††
Goldfish Swimming†
Grandpa's Farm††
Here Is the Beehive†
Here We Go A-Walking††
Hush, Little Baby†
I Am Happy†
I Am Very Special†
I Can††
I Can Hear††
I Like to Sing††
I Feed My Kitty†
I Love My Mother†
I Love the Bible††
I Will Be a Helper†
If I Were the Wind†
I'm a Little Teapot†
It's Fun to Work†
It's Time to Eat†
Jesus, Jesus, I Love Jesus†
Jesus Loves Children†
Jesus Loves Joe†
Jesus Loves Me, Jesus Loves You†
Jesus Loves You†
Jesus Was a Child††
Jimmy's Rocking†
Listen! Listen!†
Little Turtle†
Look at the Leaves††
My Family†
My Pumpkin's in the Patch††
Open, Shut Them†
Our Family††
Peekaboo†
Rain, Rain, Go Away†
Rocking My Little One†
Rocking To and Fro'†

See the Leaves Falling†
Singing Makes Me Happy†
Six Little Ducks†
Sleep, Baby, Sleep!†
Spider and Spout†
Stack the Blocks†
Star Light, Star Bright†
Teddy Bear†
Thank You, God†
Thank You, God, for Daddy†
Thank You Song††
The Bible Is a Book††
The Bus†
The Leaf Song††
What Can Billy Do?†
Where Is Thumbkin?†
You're a Special Child†

*Recordings
  Activity Songs for Tiny Tots
  Everyday Rhythms for Children
  Hymns for Quiet Times
  More Hymns for Quiet Times
  Moving Here and There
  Music for Quiet Times
  Recordings Available from Educational Activities, Inc.[2]
  Babysong
  Fingerplay Fun!
  It's Action Time—Let's Move!
  Movin'
  Pretend
  Sea Gulls . . . Music for Rest and Relaxation
  Tickly Toddle

---

[1]David Elkind, *The Hurried Child* (New York: Addison-Wesley Publishing Company, Inc., 1988 © by David Elkind), 186-191.
[2]Available from Educational Activities, Inc., P. O. Box 87, Baldwin, New York 11510 or order through the Baptist Book Store nearest you.
*Available at Baptist Book Stores or by calling toll free 1-800-458-BSSB.
†Songs from *Musical Experiences for Preschoolers; Birth Through Three.*
††Songs from *Music for Threes* (available from the Customer Service Center, 127 Ninth Avenue, North, Nashville, Tennessee 37234, or by calling toll free 1-800-458-BSSB).

12

Preparing Musical Activities for Threes

Potential Places for Musical Activities

Music is a convenient and reliable means of communicating with children. Music is highly enjoyable and makes even dull tasks seem brighter. Encourage parents and other care givers to use music with their children in daily routines. Suggest singing games for parents to teach their children. Songs can be included easily at mealtime, bedtime, while traveling, and at other family times.

Sunday School and Discipleship Training provide good opportunities to extend music activities for threes. Three-year-olds love music and enjoy church activities that involve music. Music is one reason threes look forward to coming to church. Encourage Sunday School and Discipleship Training leaders to use music in learning centers and in illustrating Bible thoughts and stories. Show these leaders how to use songs while the children are in the puzzle, block, homeliving, book, nature, and art centers. Offer suggestions of recordings to use in transition from one activity to another and during quiet times.

Church day-care leaders can use music in a variety of ways. Music makes the transition between activities smoother and helps teach basic skills. Greeting children with music, playing recordings during rest times, singing to children in the learning centers, using music with art activities, and singing during role plays and field trips are a few ways that music can be incorporated in day-care activities.

The church nursery provides a good place for children who are not involved in other church activities to be exposed to music. Some of those children are not from a musical home environment, and the musical experiences in the church nursery may be the only musical experiences they have. Teach nursery workers songs that are appropriate to sing with that age group. Give them recordings to play for the children and provide them with other music activity materials.

Plan a music activity group as a part of the preschool and children's choir schedule. In many churches, choirs meet on Wednesday or Sunday evenings when families are at church. Three-year-olds are usually in the church nursery with a loving person to care for them and their needs. This time can be led by a caring music leader, a time that offers the children an opportunity to explore the musical world.

Parent Involvement

Two approaches are recommended in developing a music activity group: leaders working with children, and leaders and parents working together with children. Parental involvement offers extra advantages. The parents' presence communicates to the children the importance of music in their lives. The carryover value of the parents' participating with the children at home in activities that they learned together in a music activity group is tremendous. When parents do attend the music sessions, encourage them to participate with the children. The benefits of observing are nothing compared to those of participating. Help them understand that they should not try to do activities *for* the children (such as taking a child's hands and playing an instrument) but should *demonstrate* activities for the children to imitate. Plan the activities each week; lead the parents in learning the activities; then allow the parents to lead the children during the music activity time.

If the parent involvement approach will not work for you, enlist an adult leader for every four or five children in the music activity group. Remember, model the activities for the children and then encourage them to do the activities. Use this sequence when presenting an activity: *tell them, show them, let them do it.* Assign each adult leader to a small-group activity.

Room Arrangement

The Sunday School room for three-year-olds has the best potential for a music activity group. Move the tables and chairs to one end of the room for individual activities and use the open space at the other end of the room for learning centers, small-group activities, and large group. *Music for Threes,*** Item 12, contains further information about room arrangement.

Place individual and small-group activities in a variety of learning centers around the room. The activities should be unstructured, allowing the children the freedom to explore and make their own discoveries. Make at least four options available to the children each week in the individual-oriented learning centers. Plan two small-group activities each week in the learning centers in addition to the unstructured exploratory activities.

Since three-year-olds are not as socially oriented as fours and fives, have plenty of supplies available in the learning centers and small groups. Younger preschoolers do not understand the concept of sharing. Having more than enough supplies for everyone will help avoid problems. When parents are present, they should participate with the children in the learning centers. Leaders and parents should lead the small-group activities.

Plan a smooth transition from the learning centers or individual activities to the small groups. Many of the activities in *Musical Experiences for Preschoolers; Birth Through Three** contain information for making successful transitions. Puzzles, blocks, homeliving, nature, music, art, and books are learning centers that can be used in individual and small-group activities. Ideas for how to use learning centers are found at the beginning of each unit in *Music for Threes*.

Free movement to music and singing are the primary activities of large group. Listening to environmental sounds and play times spent performing short dramatic plays are also appropriate. Encourage parents and leaders to participate in the large-group activities, especially movement activities, with the children. *Music for Threes* and *Musical Experiences for Preschoolers; Birth Through Three* contain many individual, small-group, and large-group activities and resources.

Scheduling

Three-year-olds have a shorter attention span than four- and five-year-olds, and their weekly music activity group should reflect this difference. Thirty minutes is usually enough time for musical activities for threes. Begin each week with free play in the learning centers and small-group areas. Move freely among the children, singing to them and chanting rhythmically about their activities. After approximately 10 minutes, move smoothly to a voluntary large-group time of 10 to 15 minutes, consisting mainly of singing and movement activities. Some children will prefer to remain in the learning centers and should be allowed to do so. They learn from what they see and hear in large group even though they may be in another area of the room. Parents often report that these children sing the large-group songs at home.

End the activity period with about 10 minutes of free play in the learning centers. Continue to watch for teachable moments with the children as you move quietly among them, singing and chanting about their activities. *Musical Experiences for Preschoolers; Birth Through Three* recommends a 30-minute time frame. *Music for Threes*, designed for churches including the music for three-year-olds group in the preschool and children's choir schedule, suggests the time frame to be as follows:

Learning center	10-15 minutes
Small-group activities	10-15 minutes
Large group	8-10 minutes
Small-group activities	10-15 minutes

Learning centers   5-10 minutes
Total   43-65 minutes

Leaders

Leaders of activity groups for threes are not choir directors.
Sitting in chairs, practicing perfect posture, and rehearsing
songs to perform is *not* appropriate for three-year-olds. A music
activity time for threes is an opportunity to expose three-year-
olds to many types of music and to provide moral and spiritual
nurture through musical experiences. The role of leaders is to
provide a positive musical and spiritual environment for the
children. Be slow to teach and quick to let them learn.

Appropriate Songs

Expose three-year-olds to appropriate songs by singing to
them. Choose songs with a variety of sounds and tonalities.
Strive for a balance of songs in major keys, minor keys, and
various modes. Select songs within the range of middle C to
second-space A. Descending melodies are preferred to ascend-
ing melodies. Songs with high beginning pitches encourage
threes to use their singing voices, while songs beginning on
low pitches usually encourage threes to use their speaking
voices.

The text should be repetitious, easily understood, relative to
the world of threes, and void of symbolism, such as "Jesus is
knocking at your heart's door." (See *How to Guide Preschoolers,* * pages 166-168, for appropriate Bible thoughts for threes.
Some appropriate Bible thoughts are in chapter 2 of this book.)

Songs for threes should be short, and the rhythmic and melodic patterns should be repetitious. Many songs for threes are
based on *sol-mi, sol-la-sol,* and *sol-la-sol-mi* intervals.
Through singing these types of songs, threes develop a musical
vocabulary that enables them to create new songs, make their
own arrangements of familiar songs, play singing games, and
experiment with a variety of vocal sounds. Sources for appropriate songs for threes include *Stepping Stones to Matching
Tones,* * *Easy Songs for Early Singers,* * Sing and Move,* *Mu-*

sic for Threes, and *Musical Experiences for Preschoolers; Birth Through Three.*

Summary
Two recommended approaches in developing a music activity group are: leaders working with children, and leaders and parents working together with children. If the parent involvement approach will not work for you, enlist an adult leader for every four or five children in the music activity group.

Use this sequence when presenting an activity: *tell them, show them, let them do it.* Be slow to teach and quick to let them learn.

The Sunday School room for three-year-olds has the best potential for a music activity group. Activities should be unstructured, allowing them the freedom to explore and make their own discoveries. Younger preschoolers do not understand the concept of sharing. Having more than enough supplies for everyone will help avoid problems.

Puzzles, blocks, homeliving, nature, music, art, and books are learning centers that can be used in individual and small-group activities. Free movement to music and singing are the primary activities of large group.

Three-year-olds have a shorter attention span than four- and five-year-olds, and their weekly music activity group should reflect this difference. Thirty minutes is usually enough time for musical activities for threes. If the preschool and children's choir schedule requires that threes meet for a longer period of time, see *Music for Threes* for additional suggestions for successful pacing of activities.

A music activity time for threes is an opportunity to expose three-year-olds to many types of music and to provide moral and spiritual nurture through musical experiences. The role of leaders is to provide a positive musical and spiritual environment for the children.

Songs for threes should be short and repetitious.

---

*Available at Baptist Book Stores or by calling toll free 1-800-458-BSSB.
**Available from the Customer Service Center, 127 Ninth Avenue, North, Nashville, Tennessee 37234, or by calling toll free 1-800-458-BSSB.

13

How Threes Respond to Music

Three-year-olds respond to music differently than older pre-schoolers and elementary-age children. Threes are different physically, mentally and emotionally, and spiritually. Remember these differences when planning their musical activities. Threes require more loosely structured music activity times than those planned for older children. Threes experience music through listening, moving, singing, and playing instruments.

Listening

Through listening activities, three-year-olds:
- Continue to listen attentively to music.
- Become aware of same and different sounds.
- Respond to fast and slow and loud and soft.

Threes enjoy listening to music and will listen attentively for short periods of time. It is common to see three-year-olds select the same recording week after week in the music learning center and ask a leader or parent to play it. Often the children will ask the adult to play the recording five or six times in succession and will simply walk or run away from the adult to another learning center when they tire of the activity. Since all younger preschoolers learn through repetition, honor their requests to hear a recording as many times as they wish. Include recordings from master composers. Bach's *Brandenburg Concerto in F Major* elicits many different musical responses (listening, moving, and vocalizing) from threes. Recordings featuring high-pitched instruments, such as violins, flutes, and harpsichord are favorites of threes.

Three-year-olds also enjoy hearing leaders and parents sing.

The ability to sing on pitch is important, but a solo quality voice is not required to sing effectively with threes. Dramatic voices with a heavy vibrato are not as interesting to threes as lighter voices with less vibrato. Threes enjoy hearing adults initiate singing conversations with them, although the conversations are usually one-sided. The children prefer adults to sing to them instead of simply talking to them. Threes also enjoy hearing leaders and parents sing instructions and greetings to them. Transitions between different activites are made smoother when adults sing to the children.

Listening Activity #1: Threes need to learn how to listen before they can participate effectively in organized listening activities. Early in the year lead threes in activities that will encourage the development of listening skills. Hide behind a table or other object or have the children close their eyes or turn their backs so that they cannot see what you are doing. Make a variety of sounds with different body instruments (clapping, snapping fingers, tapping feet on the floor), and ask individual children to identify the sound you made. Allow some of the older threes to make sounds and let the group identify the sounds they make. Repeat activities such as this for several weeks until the children are able to identify environmental sounds. As their listening skills develop, include familiar classroom instruments that have been used in learning centers and in small- and large-group activities. Allow the threes to select two or three familiar instruments to use in the game.

Listening Activity #2: Tape record sounds of familiar animals, such as dogs, cats, and cows, and play the tape. Have the children try to name the animals whose sounds they hear on the recording. Provide teaching pictures of the animals so the children can point to them as they identify the sounds they hear. With older threes, tape record some of the children or leaders singing or talking and have the other children guess the names of the children and leaders they hear on the recording. Extend this activity by making a picture with an instant-developing camera of each child and leader in the group. Have the children select the picture of children or leaders they hear on the tape. Save the pictures of the children and leaders for future activities.

Whisper instructions to threes or tell them you have a secret to share. A whisper interests and excites threes and helps them concentrate on the instructions and the activity. Encourage the children to mimic your whisper in response so they can discover the difference between their whispering and speaking voices.

Same and different sounds. Threes learn about same and different sounds in music by first learning about same and different. Show threes a group of pictures, some of which match and some that do not. Use pictures of familiar objects, such as mittens, fruit, socks, and shoes. As you display the pictures, two at a time, explain that when the pictures look alike they are the *same* and when they are not alike they are *different.* Give the children opportunities to tell you if different combinations of the pictures are the same or different. Provide these picture-matching games often for younger threes. After they are able to distinguish between pictures that are the same and pictures that are different, they are ready to begin to identify same and different sounds. However, *seeing* same and different is easier than *hearing* same and different. The visual reinforcement helps preschoolers make their decision. This activity can be used as an individual or small-group activity or as part of a learning center. Include in the book center books that deal with same and different pictures, objects, and colors. Provide same and different block shapes in the block center. Give threes the opportunity to see and feel the difference between seashells, rocks, and leaves in the nature center. Include same and different plastic food items in the homeliving center.

After learning to visually distinguish same and different items, threes can become aware of same and different sounds through listening activities. Give each child a piece of PVC pipe or a one-foot piece of dryer hose. These can be purchased at a hardware store. Have the children put one end of the pipe or hose to their ear and the other end to their mouth. Ask the children to speak or sing into the pipes. Lead them in experimenting with the vocal sounds they can make. Give them the opportunity to hear and feel the difference between whispering, speaking, singing, and outside shouting voices while using the PVC pipe or dryer hose. After most of the children have discovered the singing voice, practice echo singing with the PVC pipe or dryer hose. After the children are able to echo close intervals, such as *sol-mi*, echo sing fragments of familiar songs.

Have the children put one end of the pipe or hose to their ear and the other end to their mouth. Ask the children to speak or sing into the pipes.

Collect empty plastic, egg-shaped hosiery containers of the same color. Fill the containers with a variety of items, such as salt, uncooked macaroni, erasers, and small rocks or seashells. Seal the egg-shaped containers with duct tape, strapping tape, or other strong bonding material to prevent the contents from spilling. Be sure that some of the containers have identical contents so some of the sounds will be the same. Let the preschoolers shake the containers to find those that sound the same and those that sound different. Avoid using empty child proof medicine bottles because their use could encourage threes to play with dangerous medicine bottles from home medicine cabinets. Some persons have successfully used empty plastic 35 millimeter camera film cases by covering the cases with brightly colored clear, adhesive-backed plastic, half filling them with a variety of items, and gluing the tops on the cases. Scrub these cases thoroughly to remove any chemical residue before using them. Store the empty film cases for future use in individual listening activities, small groups, and learning centers.

Provide a variety of classroom rhythm instruments with which threes can experiment freely and hear same and different sounds. For example, put two sets of wrist bells and a hand drum together and see if threes can discover which instruments sound the same. Since they can see them, they usually realize that the wrist bells sound alike.

Later in the year when the children are familiar with the sight and sound of the instruments, play them out of the children's view and have them identify which instruments sound the same and which sound different.

Play a game with older threes in which leaders whom the children know hide. Have each leader speak to the children, and let the children guess which leader they heard speaking. As an extension of this activity, let some children hide from the leaders and other children and have the group guess which child is speaking.

Threes enjoy recording a variety of sounds. Play the tape recording for the children and let them try to remember what made the recorded sounds. Repeat the tape often. Include the sounds of body instruments, classroom instruments, leaders' and parents' voices, children speaking, and other room environmental sounds. Make different tapes throughout the year, including a tape demonstrating whispering, speaking, singing, and outside shouting voices.

Threes enjoy using a stethoscope to listen to their heartbeats and those of other children. The heartbeat is similar to the rhythmic feeling of a meter. This is often the meter to which children respond first.

Threes respond to fast and slow. Give each of the children an elephant stick puppet or finger puppet. Play slow selections from *Everyday Rhythms for Children** and have the children pretend their elephant puppets are tired as they move them slowly to the tempo of the music. Give each of the children a mouse stick puppet or finger puppet. Play fast selections from the same recording or from Baroque recordings, such as Daquin's *Le Coucou*. Have the children pretend their mouse puppets are running to the tempo of the music.

Let the children imitate you as you walk or run while listening to "Variations on a Nursery Rhyme" from *Everyday Rhythms for Children* recording. Vary the activity by slowly or quickly waving brightly colored scarves while listening to the same recording. If space is limited, have the children move only their fingers while listening to the variations.

Threes respond to loud and soft. Provide child-sized rocking chairs for threes. Have the children pretend to rock a baby, a favorite doll, or a stuffed animal toy while listening to you softly sing "Jesus Loves You."† After singing, say, "Shh! Do not wake the baby." Contrast this activity with a loud march, such as "Colonel Bogey," from *World of Marches*, Bowmar Records. Ask the children to *patsch* (pat the tops of their thighs) loudly while listening to the recording. Use the *patschen* activity instead of marching because threes do not have the body coordination and balance necessary for marching. *Patschen* is a natural activity for threes although most threes will not match the steady beat of the recording when they rock or *patsch*. Keep in mind that the purpose of the activity is to develop the loud/soft concept so do not insist on accuracy of the beat.

Show the children pictures of a variety of loud and soft sound sources, such as a fire engine siren, a roaring lion, a barking dog, a sleeping rabbit, and a tiny mouse. Imitate these environmental sounds for the children and identify those which make loud sounds and those which make soft sounds.

Moving

Movement activities are significant for threes because they experience rhythm through a variety of large- and small-muscle activities. Through movement activities, three-year-olds:

- use a variety of movements.
- continue to attempt unsuccessfully to coordinate their movements to the rhythm of the music.
- move to music with a partner.
- respond to fast and slow.
- develop new movement responses influenced by their home musical environments.

Threes learn more about music through movement than through any other musical activity. Threes can respond to and learn about rhythm, melody, form, and expression through movement activities. Include small muscle and large muscle movement activities in musical activities for threes. Use movement activities with individual children, in small groups, as transition between activities, and in large group.

Consider the differences in physical skill development between younger and older threes when planning movement activities. These differences are detailed in *Musical Experiences for Preschoolers; Birth Through Three** and in the Large Muscle Play and Small Muscle Play sections of this chapter. Study the details carefully. Understanding physical characteristics of this age group is necessary to plan activities in which the children can be successful.

Begin movement activities for threes with free, unrestricted movement. It is important to model small, controllable movements for them at first and then move to larger, freer movements. Free movement exploration is important. Children need to feel the types of movements their bodies can make before attempting to coordinate those movements with music they hear.

Threes listen attentively to music that is repeated often, becoming familiar to them. They will then attempt to move in response to what they hear. Use a variety of instruments and recordings to accompany their movement activities. Participate freely with them; if they think that parents and other care givers enjoy movement activities, they will want to imitate the adults. Observe three-year-olds' swaying, rocking, and bouncing with their knees when they hear music. Since these responses occur naturally with threes, plan to include the same movements when planning their activities.

Give threes many opportunities to move freely to music; then introduce action songs that contain organized movement activities. Some movements are done in place: swinging, swaying, rocking, clapping, and *patschen*. Other movements are done while moving: walking, running, tiptoeing, and jumping. Select tempos for their new songs and movement activities by first watching the children's individual tempos as they freely move in response to music. Take your cue from the children and choose their varying tempos instead of having them try to match a tempo you set. Repeat these action songs over several weeks, especially with younger threes, so they will have an opportunity to learn the words, the rhythm of the melody, and the melody along with the appropriate actions.

Threes enjoy holding an adult's hands and swaying or rocking to music. They also enjoy holding a favorite doll or stuffed toy and moving to music. Moving to music should be a priority activity when planning for threes. They experience rhythm patterns and expression through movement, and these experiences are important in their later development. An understanding of the importance of movement is foundational in helping threes grow and develop.

The number of children involved in a music activity group influences the success of movement activities. Since threes are not as group oriented as older preschoolers, they do not enjoy large-group activities as much as they enjoy learning centers and small-group activities. They enjoy parallel play and will sometimes talk to other children about what they are doing in the learning center, but they usually prefer to play alone. Movement activities usually interest threes and will sometimes draw them into large-group activities.

Try to anticipate potential problems when planning large-group activities for threes. Consider the room arrangement, the leaders available, the number of children, and the amount of space for movement. When making a circle formation, put several small chairs in the center of the room to keep the children from moving toward the center of the circle and getting in the way of others. Consider the amount of space necessary for threes to move to music. When there are more than ten three-year-olds in your music activity group, it will be difficult to conduct movement activities in the average size Sunday School room. In-place movement (nonlocomotor) is helpful and important, but in-space movement (locomotor) is necessary for children to experience the feeling of the steady beat and subdivided beats.

Take advantage of time-proven activities to interest children in moving to music. Using a bear puppet with "Teddy Bear"† will make the singing game come alive for threes. To encourage them to use their large muscles, let them wear wrist and ankle bells while moving to the music. Tie bells on shoestrings or other clothing and let the children wear them home to encourage movement through the week. Introduce a large, brightly colored, inflatable beach ball to a few children at a time. It attracts the attention of other children in learning centers and small groups and encourages their participation in large-group movement activities.

Large Muscle Play

Knowledge and understanding of the developmental levels of physical skills enable you to choose appropriate activities for threes. Younger threes' large muscle skills include the ability to run, tiptoe, catch and throw a large ball, and walk a straight line. Older threes' large muscle skills also include tiptoeing and jumping.

Fast and Slow. Use fast and slow movement activities as transitions between other activities. Give the children toy steering wheels. If you do not have steering wheels, let them use paper plates. Have them pretend to drive cars fast and slow around the room. Threes will *experience* the feelings of fast and slow: help them label the feelings by telling them when to go fast and when to go slow. Use the terms fast and slow often as you describe and lead them in an imaginary drive around town. Use the car activity as a transition when moving between learning centers and small or large group. Sing songs, such as "Riding in My Car,"† to them while doing the activity. Encourage them to make a high-pitched car horn "beep" sound as they move. This will help them experience using the voice in a way other than talking.

Pretend train rides are good transition activities enabling threes to experience the difference between fast and slow. Lead the children in moving around the room as a pretend train. Lead the train in moving fast and moving slow. Tell a story about the train going slowly up a hill and then fast down the other side as they move around the room. Play an eighth-note rhythm on sand blocks to sound like the train. Use visuals and other aids, such as a drawing of the front of a train engine on heavy corrugated cardboard held from behind by a leader, an engineer's hat, and a wooden train whistle. These reinforcers help capture the children's attention and will prompt them to leave their learning centers and small-group activities to join the large-group train. Encourage the children to imitate the high-pitched "whoo whoo" train whistle sound. When the train of three-year-olds stops in the large-group area for singing and more movement activities, have the children continue making the train whistle sound. Immediately, lead them in singing limited-range melodies that use the *sol-mi* interval, such as in "God Cares for You."†

God Cares for You

The children probably experienced the *sol-mi* interval when they produced the "whoo-whoo" sound.

Pretending to swim is another large muscle activity that serves as a good transition activity for threes. It also helps them feel the difference between fast and slow. They can pretend to

swim around the room. Have them take an imaginary under-
water field trip to look at fish. Encourage them to pretend to
swim in a wading pool or to play in the waves hitting the beach.

Pretending to be airplanes is a good activity to emphasize
fast and slow. Let the children pretend to be airplanes taking off
fast, flying fast and slow, landing, and slowing to a stop. To vary
the activity, cut and paint a heavy corrugated cardboard airplane for each child. Let the children hold the cardboard airplanes and pretend to fly them fast and slow during
large-group time. Provide toy airplanes in the block center and
encourage threes to pretend to fly them fast and slow.

Imitating animals or insects is an excellent fast and slow activity for threes. Give the children an opportunity to sort pictures that portray the fast and slow actions of animals or
insects; then have them imitate the fast and slow actions. Have
children sort pictures, which include a small, running mouse;
then have them run in place to pretend to get away from a big
cat or to run to food. After sorting pictures, which include a
huge, slow elephant, threes can pretend to be the elephant by
moving slowly around the room using large muscle movements like an elephant. Let them listen to a recording, such as
Everyday Rhythms for Children while moving.

Use pictures of a turtle crawling, a cow eating grass, and a
crawling worm to illustrate slow actions. Encourage the children to imitate their movements so they can experience the
concept of *slow*. Display pictures of a running rabbit, a flying
bird, and a flying bee to illustrate fast actions, and have the
children imitate them to experience the concept of *fast*. These
all are good transition activities.

Child-sized rocking chairs lend themselves to illustrating fast and slow. Secure enough child-sized rocking chairs for either a small-group experience or for large-group time, depending on the size of the music activity group and the size of the room. Provide enough adult-sized rocking chairs for the parents and their leaders. Mix the chairs in a circle formation. Have the children and adults rock while listening to recordings that illustrate fast and slow. Good recordings to use for this activity are the last movement (Allegretto—Alla Turca) of Mozart's Sonata in A Major (K. 331), "Turkish March," (fast) and J. S. Bach's "Air on the G String" (slow). Extend the activity by having the children and adults pretend to rock a baby while you sing to them, varying the tempo of the song to include obviously fast and slow examples.

From a discount store, purchase an inexpensive, brightly colored, sheer scarf for each child. Squares of chiffon or sheer fabric will work as well. Help each child find his own personal space or "bubble" in the room and give each a scarf. Play different selections from Everyday Rhythms for Children recording. Ask the adults to move their scarves fast and slow while listening to the recording and encourage the children to imitate the adults' movements.

A similar activity requires the purchase of one-foot lengths of brightly colored satin ribbon from a fabric or craft shop. Tie each ribbon to the end of a ribbed rhythm stick. (Smooth sticks do not work as well as ribbed sticks because the ribbons often slide off the end of smooth rhythm sticks.) After making sure that the space between each child is sufficient for safety, give the children the ribbon sticks. Allow the children to experiment freely with the ribbon sticks. Ask them to move the sticks fast and slow in a variety of directions. Have them wiggle the ribbons on the ground, move them from side to side, and wave them over their heads. A variation of this activity is to securely tape several ribbons to the end of empty paper towel tubes. A paper towel tube with crepe paper strips taped to the end of the tube is also effective, but it is not as durable when used by three-year-olds.

After the threes have had many opportunities to move in free exploration activities, introduce a few action songs and singing games. Songs, such as "If You're Happy" lend themselves well to many weeks of repetition. This song can be extended to include a variety of actions.

If You're Happy

*Substitute: tap your toe, nod your head, do all three.
Traditional.

Use hand puppets, finger puppets, or face masks attached to tongue depressors or large craft sticks with singing games, such as "Teddy Bear" and "The Old Gray Cat." Threes do not like to wear masks, but they enjoy holding masks in front of their faces if the masks are attached to tongue depressors. Singing games, such as "The Old Gray Cat,"† not only allow the children to experience fast and slow through large muscle movement but also require the children to use their listening skills to know which movements are appropriate.

A three-year-old enjoys having a leader watch his individual tempo as he walks across the room, the leader matching his tempo on a drum or other classroom rhythm instrument. Threes delight in teasing leaders by varying their tempo between fast and slow. It is important that the leader match the children's tempos, for they have difficulty matching a tempo

The Old Gray Cat

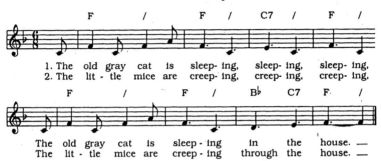

1. The old gray cat is sleep- ing, sleep- ing, sleep- ing,
2. The lit - tle mice are creep- ing, creep- ing, creep- ing,

The old gray cat is sleep - ing in the house. —
The lit - tle mice are creep - ing through the house. —

3. The little mice are nibbling . . . in the house.
4. The little mice are sleeping . . . in the house.
5. The old gray cat comes creeping . . . through the house.
6. The little mice all scamper . . . through the house.

Traditional American Song.

set by an adult. Ask the children, one at a time, to walk across the room while you play an instrument to match the rhythm of their walk. They will feel successful as they walk to the beat of the instrument.

Threes also can experience fast and slow through jumping. Demonstrate jumping fast and slow and encourage them to imitate you.

Use the movements of various other animals to encourage threes to want to participate in movement activities. Play "The Kangaroo" from *Everyday Rhythms for Children* recording to show the difference in music that makes you want to jump and music that makes you want to walk. The recording gives verbal instructions for walking and jumping fingers and then the whole body like a kangaroo. Have the children listen and respond by bending their knees on the hopping music. Add to the fun by making each child a set of kangaroo ears to wear during the activity.

Look for listening and movement selections on previous issues of the *Preschool Music Cassette* or *Preschool Music Recording*. Select those that help the children experience fast and slow. Enhance the moving activities with visuals and rhythm motivators. See *Teaching Music Concepts Through Art Activities** for additional suggestions and ideas for listening and moving activities.

Look for recordings that lend themselves to swaying and knee-bending activities. Swaying is a natural large muscle movement activity for threes, and it can be used effectively to help the children feel the concept of *slow*. Bending the knees is another natural large muscle moving activity for threes. Have the children do knee bends to feel the concept of *slow*.

Give threes the opportunity to tiptoe and run (in place) in small- and large-group activities. Through tiptoeing, threes respond to music that moves slowly. Threes can run on tiptoes as a large muscle activity. They can also run with their fingers on the floor as a small muscle activity.

Small Muscle Play

Younger three-year-olds' small muscle skills include simple uses of blunt-nosed scissors, crayons, and pencils; scribbling; and playing with blocks. Older threes use scissors, crayons, and pencils less than younger threes and also enjoy copying adults' block models rather than devising their own as they did as younger threes.

Keeping in mind the developmental differences between younger and older threes in small muscle activities, the following types of activities can be adapted for music activity groups for threes.

Fast and Slow. Threes can respond to the feeling of fast and slow through finger plays. *Musical Experiences for Preschoolers; Birth Through Three* and *Sing and Move** contain finger plays appropriate for threes. Most leaders and parents fondly remember learning finger plays, such as "Spider and Spout"† and "I'm a Little Teapot"† when they were children, and they will feel comfortable singing these and others with the children at home and at church. Finger plays, such as "Here Is the Beehive"† serve multiple purposes by encouraging the children to explore a variety of vocal sounds. The children can pretend that the bees are flying slowly as they do their finger play and make the buzzing sound with their voices. Have them pretend the bees are flying fast. Find other appropriate finger plays in the books mentioned.

Both listening and moving skills are required for appropriate small muscle responses to finger plays, such as "Open, Shut Them."†

Open, Shut Them

1. O - pen, shut them, o - pen, shut them;
2. W alk them, walk them, walk them, walk them,
3. W alk them, walk them, walk them, walk them,
4. O - pen, shut them, o - pen, shut them;

Now we'll give a clap. O - pen, shut them,
Right up to your chin. O - pen wide your
Way down to your toes. Make them jump up
Now we'll give a clap. O - pen, shut them,

o - pen, shut them; Put them in your lap.
smil - ing mouth, But do not put them in.
ver - y fast, And hit you on your nose.
o - pen, shut them; Put them in your lap.

Traditional.

"Open, Shut Them" is an excellent finger play to use in a limited space. Varying the tempo of this finger play can help the children discover the difference between fast and slow.

Songs not originally intended as finger plays can become such with a little imagination. For example, "Turtles" can be dramatized as a large muscle movement activity by the children, or it can be used as a small muscle movement finger play.

Turtles

1. Lit - tle tur-tles walk so slow,— Walk so slow— where they go;
2. Great big tur-tles creep a-long,— Creep a-long— all day long;

Lit - tle tur-tles walk so slow And nev- er make a sound.
Great big tur-tles creep a-long And nev- er make a sound.

Little turtle

Great big turtles

Threes can experience fast and slow in the block learning center. They love to play in this area and will enjoy building at varying fast and slow tempos at the encouragement of, or through the example of, adults. Recordings of music with varying tempos encourages this type of movement. Sing "Stack the Blocks"† at varying tempos to the children, and they likely will respond to your tempos as they build.

Use small toys in the block area. Have the children drive toy cars fast across a block bridge while a leader or parent sings "Riding in My Car." Then have the children drive the toy cars slowly across the block bridge. Threes can move wooden toys fast or slowly while adults sing in rhythm to their movements. While observing threes playing freely with toys in the block area, adults can label their movements as *fast* and *slow* in conversation with them: "John, your car is moving *fast* across the bridge you built."

Younger threes enjoy using crayons to scribble on paper. Provide a variety of large crayons and long sheets of white paper in or near the art area. While the children scribble on the paper, watch the tempo of their scribbling. Introduce them to the terms *fast* and *slow* by commenting to them about what you observe: "Susan, you are moving your crayon very fast."

After using the terms *fast* and *slow* in the context of art activities, add music to the activity by playing fast or slow beats on a drum or other instrument as they scribble. Spontaneously create songs about what the children say they are drawing and sing those songs at fast and slow tempos as they scribble.

Use walking fingers as a small muscle movement activity

with one or more children. Demonstrate how fingers can walk up an arm, on a table, or on the floor. Pretend that the parents or leaders are mother and father monkeys and the children are baby monkeys. The baby monkeys watch the mothers' and fathers' walking finger movements and imitate them. The fingers walk at a fast pace and then slowly without music. Then ask the children to walk their fingers while listening to the leaders sing a familiar song.

Threes like *patschen* (patting thighs). Although some large muscles are used in *patschen* activities, these activities can be considered basically small muscle activities. Threes enjoy patting fast and patting slowly with or without music. In either case, the threes experience the difference between how fast and slow feel, and the adults label the experience for the threes by commenting on what they do. Threes should not be asked to *label* the difference between fast and slow but should simply be given the opportunity to experience how different fast and slow *feel*.

Singing (Vocalizing and Chanting)

Some of the most important activities for threes include singing, vocalizing, and chanting. They experience singing, vocalizing, and chanting by:
- Beginning to sing the correct words, rhythm, and melody of a song.
- Inventing new songs.
- Making new arrangements of familiar songs.
- Playing singing games.
- Singing songs imitating animals or environmental sounds.

By the time children are three years old, they begin learning whole songs if the songs are short and repetitive. They concentrate on the words of a song first and tend to recognize a new or slightly familiar song by the words. Threes concentrate on the rhythm of the melodic line before they learn the intervals of the melody. Make as much use of each song as you can. Threes learn songs by hearing them repeated often. Vary the way you introduce songs to threes. Include techniques such as singing the melody without the words, using a neutral syllable like "loo" or "bum." The absence of words helps the children concentrate on the melody.

Vary pitch levels of chanting exercises to produce more musical sounds. Sing pure vowel sounds, linking consonant sounds between words. Threes need to hear a linked, *legato* sound in chanting (but do not use the word *legato* with them). Make chanting exercises musical experiences for them. The purpose of the exercise is to feel the rhythm of the *melodic* line, an activity which suggests varying the pitch levels of the talking voice.

The first songs sung by threes are their variations of familiar songs. After they develop a mental vocabulary of familiar sounds, they begin to create their own songs based on familiar melodic and rhythmic patterns. Many threes sing songs between the range of middle C and second-space A with accuracy. They need to explore the sounds that their voices can make outside of this range, and they need to hear songs outside of this range in preparation for later singing skill development. At this stage, however, most threes will be more successful at matching pitches within the middle C to second-space A range. Songs beginning on middle C are difficult for some children to match because middle C is a talking tone. Sometimes songs beginning in the higher part of the range, on second-space A, are difficult for threes initially.

Finding the Singing Voice. One of the first steps in helping threes find their singing voices is to help them hear the different kinds of sounds their voices can make. All threes have used the talking and shouting voices, but some of them have not understood the difference between these voices and the singing voice. Some children come from homes in which music is not an important part of the environment. Others hear low talking voices from parents and siblings at home. Some children are shy or uninterested in participating while others may be slow in physical development.

Suggestions for helping threes find their singing voices:

1. Through much repetition of a core of songs, help the children develop a "mental vocabulary" of melody and rhythm patterns from which threes' first attempts to create songs will be based. *Stepping Stones to Matching Tones** refers to this mental vocabulary as a "tonal memory bank."[1]

2. Help threes experience the head voice they need for singing by singing songs and using other activities in which animal, insect, and environmental sounds can be imitated.

3. Use visual aids to interest the children in singing and vocalizing activities.

4. Select limited-range songs for threes' singing activities.

5. Let the children hear singing at home, in the day-care center, and at church.

Repetition of a Core of Songs. Develop a core of songs from Sunday School, extended session, and other curricula for threes to be sung *to* them by leaders in a music activity group. If parents and church care givers use songs and activities in *Musical Experiences for Preschoolers; Birth Through Three,* include those songs as a part of the core of songs. For example, "Thank You, God, for Everything"† has a three-note range and begins on F above middle C, which is in the middle of a three's singing range. The song also consists of only two short phrases and uses steady and subdivided beats in the melodic rhythm. After hearing many repetitions of this song, some threes will try to imitate the song or sing their own variations of it. Since the song has short phrases, simple rhythmic patterns, and a limited range, threes should be successful in eventually learning to sing the song. From *Musical Experiences for Preschoolers; Birth Through Three,* choose other songs for threes to hear and eventually sing. Some good choices are "God Cares for You,"† "God Makes the Wind Blow,"† "Thank You, God,"† "It's Time To Eat,"† "round and round" fragments of "The Bus,"† "Teddy Bear" fragments of "Teddy Bear,"† "bow, wow, wow" fragments of "Doggy, Doggy,"† the "meow, meow, meow" fragment of "I Feed My Kitty,"† and the "quack, quack, quack" fragment of "Six Little Ducks."† From *Music for Threes,*** select five songs to use each week in the music activity time. Good selections from *Music for Threes* are "Grandpa's Farm,"†† "Farm Friends,"†† "Thank You, God,"†† "Thank You Song,"†† and the "meow" phrase of "God Loves Me."†† *Imitating Sounds and Using Visual Aids.* Threes learn to find the head voice by singing songs and participating in activities in which they imitate animal, insect, and other environmental sounds. Songs in *Musical Experiences for Preschoolers; Birth*

Through Three, such as "Doggy, Doggy," "Here Is the Beehive," ".I Feed My Kitty," "If I Were the Wind," and "Six Little Ducks," can easily be used to encourage threes to imitate animal, insect, and environmental sounds in the songs. *Music for Threes* contains similar songs, such as "Farm Animals," "Farm Friends," and "God Loves Me."

Puppets that illustrate these kinds of songs can be used successfully with threes to interest the children in singing activities. For example, a cat hand puppet interests threes in producing the "meow" sound in "I Feed My Kitty." A bear hand puppet interests threes in participating in and eventually singing the "Teddy Bear" fragments of "Teddy Bear." A cow hand puppet encourages threes to sing the "moo, moo" fragment of "Farm Animals." A dog puppet used to illustrate a woofing sound also can be used to illustrate "Doggy, Doggy" and its "bow, wow, wow" phrases.

Imitating a hooting owl can be enhanced by giving the threes pairs of owl wings and allowing them to flap their wings as they make the hooting sound. Other sounds that threes can imitate that will help them find their singing voices are sirens, train whistles, and the "beep, beep" sound of a car horn. These sounds can be used as part of a transition activity between other activities.

Selecting Limited-Range Songs for Threes. All songs included in Sunday School, extended session, and preschool music materials are not intended to be sung *by* three-year-olds. The ranges of some songs extend beyond the middle C to second-space A range that is comfortable for threes. Songs such as these are designed to be sung *by* adults *to* threes. Part of the process in learning to talk is being immersed in a language environment. Regional speech sounds result from these early years of exposure to language. Threes learn to expand their vocabularies by imitating what they hear adults say. Likewise, part of the process in learning to sing is being immersed in a musical environment. Threes learn to find their singing voices by imitating the singing sounds they hear adults make.

Choose and repeat songs often that lie within the middle C to second-space A range so the children will have some success in singing. Note which songs parents report their threes singing at home. Also choose some songs to sing *to* the children that will expose them to sounds that exceed the middle C to second-space A range, so they will be familiar to the children as their ranges expand. *Musical Experiences for Preschoolers; Birth Through Three, Easy Songs for Early Singers,* * *Sing and Move, Stepping Stones to Matching Tones,* and *Music·for Threes* are good resources for songs within the middle C to second-space A range and for other songs appropriate for use with threes.

Singing for Threes. Threes should hear parents sing at home and teachers sing in the day-care center and in other church activities. Share the core curriculum of songs you developed with parents for home use and with the church day-care center for use in their daily routine. These familiar songs will help threes feel safe in their environment and will reinforce musical and spiritual growth. Help parents and day-care leaders learn the songs and feel comfortable singing them. Give them sample activities of how to use the songs.

Playing Instruments

Experimenting with instruments and other sound sources is important in the musical development of threes. They should explore a variety of environmental sounds, homemade instruments, and classroom instruments.

Instruments can be used in several ways in a music activity group. They can be used as a part of music and art learning centers, in small-group activities, in illustrating stories and songs in large group, and in role-playing activities.

Introduce threes to homemade and classroom instruments through body instruments. Threes enjoy clapping, stomping, rubbing their hands together, patting their knees, hitting the floor with their hands, making tongue noises, and making other percussive body sounds. A favorite game for threes, using body instruments, is to watch and imitate a parent or an adult leader. When the adult claps, the children clap. If the adult makes tongue noises, the children attempt to make the same tongue noises. Body instruments can be used with singing games and fun songs as well. Two songs, "Can You Clap

Your Hands?"† and "If You're Happy," specify clapping but can easily be adapted to include other body instruments.

Environmental Sound Sources. Another step in introducing homemade and classroom instruments to threes is to allow them to experiment with a variety of environmental sounds. They are still enticed by pots and pans. Place pots and pans and plastic cooking utensils in the homeliving and music learning centers. When the children beat the pots and pans, sing songs, such as "What Can Billy Do?," substituting a child's name for "Billy," and "plays the pan" or "plays the lid" for "drinks his milk." Provide other environmental sound sources by putting crunchy, dry fall leaves or dried beans in empty, plastic butter containers.

Homemade Instruments

After introducing threes to body instruments and experimenting with environmental sounds, introduce them to homemade instruments they can take home. These instruments can be made in advance by leaders, or they can be made by parents and children in an art learning center. Because of the short attention span and small muscle coordination of threes, adults will usually do most of the construction of the instruments. Realizing this, do most of the construction before the music activity group meets. Make tambourines from two paper plates, yarn, and metal washers. Place one plate facedown on top of the other plate. Punch holes around the edges of the plates with a single hole punch. Thread the yarn through each hole in the plates and through the middle of a metal washer at each hole, tying the yarn when threaded through the last hole in the plates.

Make triangles from metal coat hangers, bending down the top of the hangers to form a metal loop. Thread a piece of yarn through the metal loop and tie the ends of the yarn together in a secure knot. Hold the coat hanger triangle by the yarn and use a metal spoon as a striker.

Make rhythm sticks by cutting 12-inch lengths of -inch wooden dowel rods. Sand the ends of the sticks to avoid getting splinters in the children's hands. These inexpensive sticks can be used in singing games, imitation games, movement activities, and many other activities.

Make drums of various timbres from different materials. Cover empty oatmeal boxes with brightly colored, adhesive-backed plastic or white art paper that the children have decorated. Tape the oatmeal box top to the box before covering the box with the adhesive-backed plastic or art paper. Empty coffee cans, empty plastic whipped topping containers, and large plastic storage containers with lids also can be used as drums.

Make maracas in the art learning center or the music learning center. Place dried beans or rice in small plastic eggs (or egg-shaped panty hose containers) to make maracas. Tape the

eggs with clear packing tape to prevent spilling the beans. Let the threes take the egg maracas home with them to use when listening to music at home.

Make sand blocks by cutting one-by-three-by-six-inch pieces of wood and attaching a drawer knob or empty thread spool to the center of each piece. Paint the blocks bright colors and staple a three-by-six-inch piece of sandpaper to each piece of wood on the side opposite the drawer knob or spool. Use these sand

blocks as part of a transition activity while singing "Engine, Engine, Number Nine."† Make the sand blocks in the art learning center during a music activity time in which the sand blocks will be featured in several activities.

Commercially produced wrist bells do not fit preschoolers' wrists. Individualize wrist bells for each three-year-old by purchasing ⅛-inch elastic banding and jingle bells from a craft store. Thread the elastic through the tops of the jingle bells and tie the ends together to form a wrist bell, giving each child an individual fitting. To make wider width wrist bells, sew jingle bells onto ¾-inch elastic. Sew the ends of the elastic together to fit the wrist of each child.

After introducing threes to body instruments, environmental sound sources, and homemade instruments, let them experiment freely with classroom instruments in the music learning center. Feature different types of instruments each week to create interest among the children. Provide enough classroom rhythm instruments each week for several children to play simultaneously. Since threes do not yet understand the concept of sharing, problems will occur if enough instruments are not provided for all the children.

Occasionally, plan a small-group activity near the music center that will involve classroom instruments. Demonstrate the proper use of the classroom rhythm instruments and monitor the music center when the instruments are being used. Avoid instruments, such as jingle clogs, that are potentially dangerous to threes. The jingle clog has a large nail protruding upward that could cause an eye injury or serious cut when used incorrectly. Consider introducing classroom rhythm instruments in the music learning center by types—whether they are struck, scraped, or shaken.

Include the Autoharp in the music learning center. Give threes a variety of strummers, such as a rubber doorstop, a

large eraser, a comb, and a spatula. A leader or parent should monitor the use of the Autoharp so that the instrument is not dropped or broken. While a child strums, press the chord bars and sing a song that is being used in large-group singing experiences that month. You can find information about playing the Autoharp and using the Autoharp to teach musical concepts in *Using the Autoharp with Preschoolers and Children.**

Include resonator bells and step bells occasionally in the music learning center. Resonator bells can be used easily in group play because individual resonator bells and mallets can be distributed to several children simultaneously. Threes can also experiment freely with the variety of sounds the different resonator bells make. Individual children can play the step bells and begin experiencing pitches moving up or down or staying the same aurally and visually.

The glockenspiel is a good choice for the music learning center. The tone bars are metal, and the instrument is smaller than the xylophone and metallophone. Let threes experiment freely with their sound. Song bells are fairly inexpensive, xylophone-like mallet instruments that make good additions to a music learning center.

Illustrating Stories and Songs. Use instruments in large group to interest children in stories and songs and to illustrate the texts. Parents or leaders can make telling "God Made the Birds," page 79, Chapter 10, much more interesting by playing finger cymbals whenever the word *bird* is read. Illustrate other words in the story with other instruments: sand blocks (nest), drum (eggs), and wrist bells (baby bird). Use the instruments with the story only after the story is familiar to the threes; otherwise, they will concentrate on the instruments more than on the words.

Enhance singing games, such as "The Old Gray Cat,"† by using finger cymbals to represent the cat and a tambourine to represent the little mice. The use of instruments is especially effective when using stick puppets with the song. Toward the end of the year, some threes will enjoy using instruments in role-playing activities led by parents or leaders. Think of ways to use other instruments to enhance stories, songs, and books in small- and large-group activities. "Goldilocks and the Three

Bears" and "Chicken Little" are excellent stories for such treatment.

Summary

The combined influences of the musical environment at home, the day-care center, and church will determine the development of singing skills in threes.

Threes experience music through listening, moving, singing, and playing instruments. Through listening activities, three-year-olds become aware of same and different sounds and respond to fast and slow and loud and soft. Movement activities are significant for threes because they experience rhythm through a variety of large and small muscle activities. Through movement activities, threes continue to attempt to coordinate their movement to the rhythm of the music, move to music with a partner, respond to fast and slow, and develop new movement responses. They learn more about music through movement than through any other musical activity. They can respond to and learn about rhythm, melody, form, and expression through movement activities.

Some of the most important activities for threes include singing, vocalizing, and chanting. They experience singing, vocalizing, and chanting by beginning to sing the correct words, rhythm, and melody of a song, inventing new songs; making new arrangements of familiar songs; playing singing games; and singing songs imitating animals or environmental sounds. By the time children are three years old, they begin learning whole songs if the songs are short and repetitive. They concentrate on the words of a song first and tend to recognize a new or slightly familiar song by the words. They concentrate on the rhythm of the melodic line before they learn to sing the intervals of the melody.

Experimenting with instruments and other sound sources is important in the musical development of threes. Instruments can be used in several ways in a music activity group. They can be used as a part of music and art learning centers, in small-group activities, in illustrating stories and songs in large group, and in role-playing activities.

Resources

Andress, Barbara. "Music for Every Stage." *Music Educators Journal.* 76 (October 1989): 22-27.

Edge, Rhonda J. *Musical Experiences for Preschoolers; Birth Through Three.* Nashville: Convention Press, 1989.

Kenney, Susan. "Music Centers: Freedom to Explore." *Music Educators Journal.* 76 (October 1989): 32-36.

McDonald, Dorothy C. and Gene M. Simons. *Musical Growth and Development: Birth Through Six.* New York: Macmillan, Inc., 1988.

Scott, Carol Rogel. "How Children Grow—Musically." *Music Educators Journal.* 76 (October 1989): 28-31.

Strickland, Jenell. *How to Guide Preschoolers.* Nashville: Convention Press, 1982.

Waldrop, C. Sybil. *Understanding Today's Preschoolers.* Nashville: Convention Press, 1982.

---

[1]Betty Bedsole and Derrell Billingsley, *Stepping Stones to Matching Tones* (Nashville: Broadman Press, 1979), 4.

*Available from Baptist Book Stores or by calling toll free 1-800-458-BSSB.

**Available from the Customer Service Center, 127 Ninth Avenue, North, Nashville, Tennessee 37234, or by calling toll free 1-800-458-BSSB.

+Songs from *Musical Experiences for Preschoolers; Birth Through Three.*

++Songs from *Music for Threes.*

14

Leading Musical Activities for Threes

Expectations

For the convenience of parents and leaders, music for three-year-olds often is included as a part of the preschool and children's choirs schedule. Some churches refer to this group as Music for Threes, named after the curriculum materials for three-year-olds published by the Sunday School Board. Regardless of the name chosen to identify the music activity time for three-year-olds, keep in mind that it is a music activity time as opposed to an organized choir. Failure to remember that difference will result in frustration for the leaders, parents, and children. Expect the children to enjoy the freedom of choosing activities in which they want to participate with leaders or parents. Do not expect them to enjoy sitting quietly in structured activities when developmentally they cannot remain still. Lay the foundation for more formal learning when they are older by providing a variety of singing, listening, movement, and instrumental activities in which the children can participate. Expect parents who participate to be uncomfortable at the beginning of the year, especially with movement activities. Help the parents overcome their anxiety by providing a relaxed environment and being enthusiastic.

Many parents would like to provide music activities at home for threes but do not know how. Refer them to *Musical Experiences for Preschoolers; Birth Through Three** and recordings and song collections listed in this book. Teach the parents unfamiliar songs or tape record the songs for the parents.

Music can be used with threes in Sunday School, Discipleship Training, and the church nursery to enhance Bible thoughts the children are learning and will help the children learn basic spiritual truths. Help the teachers and workers in these organizations learn how to use music effectively in their work with threes. Guide them in selecting and learning appropriate songs. Provide them with a list of suggested resources.

Decisions

What to Do with the Children—Make activity choices based on the number of children, parents, and leaders involved, and the facilities in which you meet. Vary some activities each week but include some familiar favorites of the children. Plan small-group activities to coordinate with learning centers.

Pacing—Watch the reactions of the children as they participate in activities. Be mindful of the pace you set. Even more so, be mindful of the pace the children set for themselves. Give them time to complete an activity to their satisfaction. Be flexible in the execution of your plans. Plan more activities than you anticipate needing in case the children do not respond well to some of them. If most of the children begin leaving large group before you have finished your plan, you are through. Let them go back to the learning centers and small groups.

How to Teach a Song—Sing unaccompanied to the children and sing some songs on a neutral syllable, such as "moo," "loo," or "bum," so the children can concentrate on the melody. Threes listen to the words before they hear rhythm and melody. Hearing songs without words will enhance their ability to match pitch.

Introduce only two or three songs each week. Sing a new song in its entirety before singing it in phrases. Repeat the entire song several times after learning it by phrases. Repeat songs over several weeks so that the children have opportunity to thoroughly learn the melody.

Relating to Threes—Show love to the children. Three-year-olds imitate adults' actions. What you *are* speaks louder to them than what you say. Treat them as you want to be treated.

Three-year-olds do not yet understand that other people have feelings. They see no reason why they should share their toys. Avoid problems between children by having plenty of supplies for activities and by providing plenty of space for movement. Keep their attention by singing some songs without words, playing a rhythm instrument, using puppets, and whispering or singing instructions.

Summary
Make music a vital part of the environment of threes. This includes the home, the church nursery, Sunday School, Discipleship Training, the day-care center, and music activity groups. Some churches involve parents in these groups, while others choose to involve only adult leaders. Plan individual and small-group activities in the puzzle, block, homeliving, nature, music, art, and book learning centers. Large-group activities include singing, listening, movement, and dramatic play. Leaders serve as activity leaders rather than choir directors. Unaccompanied songs are sung by adults to the children and by the children. Teach appropriate texts; select songs with repeated rhythmic and melodic patterns. Plan flexible activities according to the developmental characteristics of threes, the number of children and adults involved, the facilities, and the type approach used. Love the children at all times.

Resources
Core List of Songs from *Musical Experiences for Preschoolers; Birth Through Three** and *Music for Threes***

A Helper†
Bye, Baby Bunting†
Can You Clap Your Hands?†
Children, Obey Your Parents+
Engine, Engine, Number Nine†
Everybody Loves Baby†
God Cares for You†
God Gives Rain†
God Helps Me†
God, We Thank You†
Hush, Little Baby†

I Am Happy†
I Am Very Special†/††
I Can Help
I Like My Church†
I Love My Mother†
I Took a Trip†
I Will Sing to God†
It's Fun to Work†
It's Time to Eat†
Jesus, Jesus, I Love Jesus†
Jesus Loves Children†
Jesus Loves Joe†
Jesus Loves Me, Jesus Loves You†
Jimmy's Rocking†
Jumping! Jumping!†
Listen! Listen!†/††
Little Turtle†
My Family†
Pitter, Patter, Pit†
Rain, Rain, Go Away†
Riding in My Car†
Ring Around the Rosy†
Roll Over†
See the Leaves Falling†
Sing About Jesus†
Six Little Ducks†
Snowing†
Stack the Blocks†
Star Light, Star Bright†
Teddy Bear†
Thank You, Dear God†
Thank You, God†/††
Thank You, God, for Daddy†
Thank You, God, for Everything†
The Bus†
The Doctor Is My Friend†
The Old Gray Cat†
What Can Billy Do?†
You're a Special Child†/††

*Recordings
   Activity Songs for Tiny Tots
   Easy Songs for Early Singers
   Everyday Rhythms for Children
   Hymns for Quiet Times
   More Hymns for Quiet Times
   Moving Here and There
   Music for Quiet Times
   Songs for the Young Child
Recordings Available from Educational Activities, Inc.[1]
   Fingerplay Fun!
   It's Action Time—Let's Move!
   Movin'
   Pretend
   Sea Gulls . . . Music for Rest and Relaxation
   Tickly Toddle
Recordings of the Classics
   Brandenburg Concertos, J. S. Bach
   Symphony No. 6 in F Major ("Pastoral"), Beethoven
   Piano Sonata No. 8 in C minor, Op. 13 ("Pathetique"), 2nd
     movement, Beethoven
   "Toreador Song" from *Carmen*, Bizet
   "La Mer," Debussy
   Prelude to The Afternoon of a Faun, Debussy
   Grand Canyon Suite, Grofe
   Symphony No. 94 in G major (Surprise), Haydn
   Eine kleine Nachtmusik, Mozart
   Overture to *The Marriage of Figaro*, Mozart
   Pictures at an Exhibition, Mussorgsky
   Bolero, Ravel
   "Flight of the Bumblebee," Rimsky-Korsakov
   Overture to *William Tell*, Rossini
   Carnival of the Animals, Saint-Saens
   The Nutcracker, Tchaikovsky
   Recordings Available from Kimbo Records[2]
   Bean Bag Activities
   Playtime Parachute Fun
   Simplified Rhythm Stick Activities
   Singing Games for Little People

[1]Available from Educational Activities, Inc., P. O. Box 87, Baldwin, New York 11510, or order through the Baptist Book Store nearest you.

[2]Available from Kimbo Educational, 10 North Third Avenue-B, Long Branch, New Jersey 07740, or order through the Baptist Book Store nearest you.

*Available from Baptist Book Stores or by calling toll free 1-800-458-BSSB.

**Available from the Customer Service Center, 127 Ninth Avenue, North, Nashville, Tennessee 37234, or by calling toll free 1-800-458-BSSB.

†Songs from *Musical Experiences for Preschoolers: Birth Through Three.*

††*Songs from Music for Threes.*

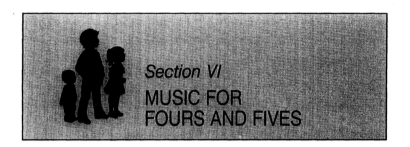

15

Preparing for Preschool Choir

Preparing Self

The prayerful acceptance of the responsibility for leading a preschool choir is the first of many preparatory steps. Accepting a new challenge is usually easier than living with the commitment to that challenge. *Webster's Ninth New Collegiate Dictionary* speaks of *commitment* in terms of "obligation" and of being "emotionally impelled." The degree of your commitment to lead a preschool choir will determine the success or failure of that leadership role and the degree to which the preschoolers' needs are met. Sacrifices will be made; expect them. Accepting the challenge of leading preschoolers is accepting the obligation to meet the challenge.

Your personal commitment and that of your preschoolers and their parents will be tested in several areas. Some of these areas are:

- Attendance

There will be times when you must choose between attending a planning meeting, a scheduled time with the preschoolers, a training session, and something you had really rather do instead. Establishing a list of priorities is helpful in developing good leadership skills. Determine the importance of your other interests and activities that might possibly interfere with your leadership responsibilities and assign each of them a priority rating. Health problems and unexpected, unscheduled family responsibilities will invariably take you away. If for no other reason, this makes your planning times necessary to prepare other leaders to substitute effectively. Faithfulness in planning determines your success and effectiveness as a leader.

• Training

A commitment to improvement should be an ongoing part of your life-style. Just as preschoolers must practice a new skill to gain ownership of that skill, so you must practice and seek new ways to gain ownership of new teaching skills. Training for preschool choir comes in four types: orientation, on-the-job training, leadership training events, and personal study.

Orientation begins as your music director or choir coordinator introduces you to new materials, equipment, and facilities. It continues as you remain alert to new ideas, teaching aids, and other helps in music and early childhood education.

On-the-job training happens as you lead the preschoolers in musical experiences, assist other leaders, observe other leaders with the children, and observe the children in musical experiences and at other times.

Leadership training events are offered frequently by local churches, associations, and state conventions. Your music director should have information on such events. The Church Music Department of the Sunday School Board provides Convention-wide music leadership conferences each summer at Ridgecrest and Glorieta Baptist Conference Centers. A variety of classes is offered for leaders in all age groups in all phases of the Music Ministry. Conference dates and information are available by writing Ridgecrest Baptist Conference Center, P. O. Box 128, Ridgecrest, North Carolina 28770; Glorieta Baptist Conference Center, P. O. Box 8, Glorieta, New Mexico 87535; or the Church Music Department.

Church music seminars are offered annually at the Church Program Training Center of the Sunday School Board in Nashville, Tennessee. These seminars offer intense study in specific areas of emphasis. Address your request for a *Church Program Training Center Catalog* to: Church Program Training Center, P. O. Box 24001, Nashville, Tennessee 37203.

Several seminaries offer church music workshops annually. These seminars are academic in nature, and the more skilled leaders in your church would profit from this professional study. Write to the seminary in your area for information.

Individual study resources are available through the Church Music Study Course System. Diplomas are awarded to those persons completing six study courses in an area of training. Course materials may be studied in a group setting or individually. Requirements for completing a specific course are given in the individual textbook. See page 222 for information about receiving credit for studying *How to Lead Preschoolers in Musical Activities*. Every choir leader should participate in one or more individual studies each year.

• Integrity

Commitment to sound teaching principles, holding firmly to spiritual truths, and practicing musical integrity are the proper attitudes for approaching the responsibility of leading preschoolers, for they deserve the best you have. Selection and preparation of materials used in guiding preschoolers require careful evaluation. Be concerned with song texts. Evaluate each song for biblical accuracy and doctrinal soundness. Be equally concerned with the musical integrity, examining the melodic range, melodic movement, rhythmic patterns, and number of syllables per beat.

• The Child

Know each preschooler individually. Teaching approaches that work with one child may or may not work with another. Teachers have different teaching styles, and learners have different learning styles. Strive to adapt your teaching styles to complement each child's learning style. Keep the needs of each child in mind when preparing activities.

Be slow to embrace new fads and avoid using clichés in your teaching. Yet, be careful not to shut yourself off from new, valid approaches. Investigate new methods and ideas. Question, weigh, and evaluate them carefully, gleaning from them techniques that will work for you and your preschoolers.

• The Learning Environment

Commitment to preparing and maintaining the preschool choir and resource center is a commitment of *time*. Preparing teaching materials, planning for storage and use of teaching materials, and sharing supplies and equipment require coordination and dedication. Whether you work in a large church with a choir coordinator and many other choir directors and leaders or in a small church where you are the only leader of a mixed-age preschool choir you must still be committed to preparing the learning environment for optimum use. Teachable moments are more likely to occur in a room where the stage is carefully set for learning and developing new skills.

Preparing the Room

The room used for making music with fours and fives will impact the learning that takes place within its walls. The room should be large enough to accomodate moving activities. An atmosphere of learning should exist; the response that a room invokes in both leaders and learners will affect the way learning takes place. The way it is decorated influences learning; color on the walls affects learning.

According to an article by Charles Businaro in *The Quarterly Review*, color can cause us to feel warm or cool, happy or depressed; inspire us to worship; motivate us to be receptive to instruction; and help us feel welcome.[1] Staying in spaces for long periods of time can cause a strong reaction if the color environment is too saturated, intense, or simply a color we find objectionable. Yellow, blue, tan, and green are usually easier to accept for long periods of time.[2] The color scheme selected for a preschool choir should have a light reflectance value of about 70 percent to give maximum learning light. The color chosen should be considered for not only how it looks by itself without activity but also how well it serves as a backdrop for the educational process.[3] In an article published in the September 17, 1973, issue of *Time* magazine, "reference was made to the work of Henner Ertel, director of an institute for rational psychology at Munich. A three-year study was conducted among children to judge, if not measure, the impact of environmental color on learning capacity. Rooms with low ceilings were painted in different colors. The better and more popular colors were light blue, yellow, yellow-green, and orange. In these environments IQ could be raised as much as 12 points. So-called ugly colors—white, black, brown—caused a drop in IQ."[4] "Researchers found that the popular colors also stimulated alertness and creativity; white, black, and brown playrooms made children duller."[5] Mr. Businaro gives the following suggestions to consider before selecting the color scheme for a preschool learning environment:

- Walls and floors need to form a backdrop or canvas for teaching. Consider teaching materials that will be used in this area. . . .
- Existing conditions, such as flooring and equipment, that remain should be considered.
- A large, uncluttered wall might be a lighter or darker color to create an understated accent wall. Hopefully, this wall will be seen as one enters the room.
- Bulletin boards or corkboards should blend with wall color when possible.
- Easily washable and low maintenance paint and material should be used. Some colors and shades of color show soil more than others.

Usually choir leaders are assigned a room with the color scheme already in place. However, if the church buildings and grounds committee is considering a change or is agreeable to a change, the suggestions from *The Quarterly Review* article should be discussed with them. In any case, changes should be made if the environment is not conducive to learning.

Usually, the same space used by other preschool organizations of the church will be the most appropriate space for preschool choir. Each organization using the room will need storage space for materials and supplies and a place for shared supplies, such as crayons and scissors. Each organization will need display space for teaching materials. One solution is to assign one of the four walls to each organization. This allows each group using the room to have a place where materials can be left on display for a unit of study or even a quarter of focus ideas. Another solution is to clear or cover bulletin boards after each use, making them ready for the next organization. Consider a portable bulletin board that can be moved in and out as needed. A folding cardboard cutting board, like those used by seamstresses for cutting fabric, will work well as a portable bulletin board. The cutting board can be covered with self-adhesive plastic or a large piece of paper and decorated to meet your needs.

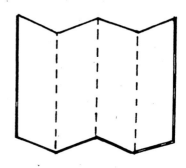

When sharing a room, the leaders of the different organizations should discuss procedures and develop a mutual understanding about how the room will be used. Preschoolers need to hear the same messages each time they enter *their* room. Consistent procedures and practices, such as where to place coats and rules for bathroom use, give preschoolers a sense of stability and security. Keeping the room neat and ready to use should be each organization's responsibility. A good guideline to consider is for each leader to be responsible for returning all equipment to its original place. A chart with the basic room arrangement might be kept on a cabinet door or beside the light switch to help in restoring the room to its original arrangement.

Many churches have budget money for purchasing supplies and equipment for preschool choirs. Learn your church's procedures for making budget requests and spending the money allocated for preschool choir.

Before making budget requests, review your teaching goals for the year. They will help you determine the equipment and supplies needed. Make a list of equipment and supplies already available; then determine what additional items should be purchased. Some of the items may include an Autoharp, resonator bells, a record player, paper, and crayons. A comprehensive inventory of items on hand plus the list of needed materials, supplies, and equipment show careful thought and stewardship of resources (see chapter 6 for a complete listing). Including sources and costs for the items requested will be helpful to the choir coordinator, church music director, and budget committee.

Some churches do not budget for the expenses of the Music Ministry. In those churches, other strategies to obtain the needed funds may be necessary. Some churches receive a special offering to meet specific needs. Others create designated funds and encourage members to give for a particular cause. These two popular practices have worked well for many churches.

A lack of budgeted funds for the operation of your preschool choir should not be a major deterrent. Many parents will give time and energy to building shelves, tables, cabinets, and other equipment to ensure a rewarding experience for their preschoolers in choir.[7]

Appropriating the Time

The time scheduled for choir is usually determined in coordination with other church activities. In determining the best time for preschool choir, the director and other leaders should be aware of the needs of the preschoolers and their families so they can select a time best suited for the preschoolers.

Preschool choirs frequently meet at the end of a busy day. Some preschoolers may have been to day-care or kindergarten and may not have been home since early morning. Others may arrive for choir immediately following a hurried meal in the church fellowship hall or in the back seat of a car via the fast-food drive-through after day-care. The preschoolers are then thrust into a learning environment.

Since the energy level of a preschooler is high immediately following a meal, plan to exercise away some of the "wiggles" the first few minutes of choir. Then perhaps a few moments of rest before asking them to absorb new information and instructions will help both the leaders and the children.

Some children will appear tired while others appear energetic. Digesting food causes both types of reactions. Meeting the needs of all preschoolers requires careful, deliberate planning. If plans are not made to meet the diverse needs of preschoolers in the early part of the rehearsal, the remaining time may not be productive.

Having a set routine to greet the arriving children can help maintain a sense of stability in the room. Early arrivers may be guided into activities that are appropriate for their level of energy at that particular time. Having a leader greet the preschoolers individually at the door as they arrive to determine the physical state of each person is helpful.

The curriculum in *The Music Leader*** is designed for small-group activities during the first 20 or 25 minutes of choir, followed by a 20-minute large-group time. Choir is preceded by early-arriver activities for those who come to the room before the scheduled time to begin. If you use this approach, your schedule would look like this:

Preschool Choir Schedule

7-10 minutes:	Early-arriver activities
20-25 minutes:	Small-group activities
20 minutes:	Large-group activities

An early-arriver activity is usually taken from either the small-group activities listed for the current unit or from the rehearsal procedures for large group. An effective early-arriver activity is one which permits arriving children to participate immediately without stopping the activity to start over each time a child arrives. If all the preschoolers arrive early, plan for two or three brief activities lasting no more than two or three minutes each to help them focus their attention on making music together. Begin with something familiar, such as a favorite singing game or a review of a song learned the previous week. Additional activities might include a physical challenge to "capture the wiggles," such as marching to the steady beat of a recording; a quiet, reflective activity, such as listening to a story from *Music Time;*** or listening to a new song that will be used later in the hour. This transitional period should last from 7 to 10 minutes; the preschoolers should then be ready for bodies and minds to begin new learning experiences in small groups. A leader should remain at the door to greet late arrivers, while other leaders join the preschoolers in a beginning large-group time.

The rehearsal procedures in the preschool units in *The Music Leader* vary from month to month, depending on the writer of the unit and the goals for the unit. Basically, the rehearsal procedures consist of small group and large group, with the small-group activities preceding the large-group activities. However, the curriculum materials are prepared for the director and leaders to use to their preschoolers' best advantage. How the curriculum materials are applied is left to the discretion of the leaders in the local church. Some churches depend heavily on early-arriver activities while other churches seldom ever need them. The suggestions in this chapter regarding rehearsal procedures are rather general and are given in the spirit of "this has worked well for some; perhaps it will work well for you."

Preschool choirs in some churches have two large-group times. The first large-group time includes two or three activities lasting no more than two or three minutes each.

Moving the preschoolers from small-group activities to the large group can be done by moving from group to group, singing a favorite marching, walking, or skipping song and leading the group to the large-group area. Give the preschoolers time to adjust to the different types of responses expected from them in large group; this transition should take from two to three minutes. Their schedule looks something like this:

7—10 minutes:	Early-arriver activities
5—10 minutes:	Transitional activities in large group
20—25 minutes:	Small-group activities
15—20 minutes:	Second large group

Whatever your approach or schedule, keep these factors in mind:

- Keep the preschoolers actively involved.
- Consider the limitations of the preschoolers' bodies.
- Blend movement and nonmovement activities.
- Allow the preschoolers to determine the conclusion of an activity.
- Remember that preschoolers will sometimes take *more* time to complete an activity than you have planned or sometimes take *less* time to complete an activity than you have planned.

- Keep in mind that a number of factors determine how long four- or five-year-olds can concentrate on one activity.
- Plan for early finishers.
- Plan adequate time for late finishers.
- Provide closure as a necessary part of the learning process.

Read chapter 7 for more detailed information on planning for preschool choir.

Pacing—moving from one activity to another—should be planned to allow for maximum involvement of everyone. Plan a variety of activities to meet the physical needs of the children. Fours and fives like to tell others in the group what reactions they are having to the learning that is happening. Guiding the responses of the children is important in evaluating how the preschoolers are perceiving what they are experiencing. Encourage "turn-taking" activities in small-group time where the preschoolers can have a turn more often. For a preschooler, waiting for 15 other children to have a turn before he gets another is like an eternity. To ensure that each preschooler has a turn to express his ideas, consider using a "waiting-a-turn" can. Write the preschoolers' names on cards or craft sticks and place them in a can. Choose names from the "waiting-a-turn" can and place them in the "had-a-turn" can so the children all get turns fairly.

Preparing Learning Experiences

How fours and fives learn.

"A preschooler learns through his five senses: hearing, touching, tasting, smelling, and seeing. Of the five senses, hearing, touching, and seeing play the lead role in the music-learning process."[8] Learning occurs when the preschooler is able to internalize, or gain ownership, of the external experiences planned for him. Learning moves from the known to the unknown, based on concrete, tangible experiences. New musical and spiritual ideas are learned through active experiences in which he can hear, feel, and see these principles at work."[9]

In *Understanding Today's Preschoolers*,* Sybil Waldrop states that we need to "constantly assess a child's needs and plan how to match toys, materials, and activities to meet his needs."[10] The following chart from *Understanding Today's Pre-schoolers* shows the appropriate types of skills, materials, and activities for fours and fives.

SKILLS AND ACTIVITIES[10]

FOUR YEARS

Skills	*Play Materials/Activities*
Skips and jumps and runs with ease	Tricycle
Engages in imaginary games	Simple games
Solves own problems usually	Walking boards, barrels
Speaks fluently; uses broad concepts (month, next summer)	Art materials (pencils, crayons, paint, clay)
Matches pictures	Climbing apparatus
Is an accurate observer	Blocks (variety of unit
Asks innumerable questions	blocks)
Perceives analogies	Sings with group usually
Can conceptualize and generalize	Books
Can participate in a short group time	Stories
Is almost self-dependent in routines of home life	Pictures (variety; some
Recognizes different forms	puzzle pictures)
Climbs with ease	Opportunities to categorize
Plays cooperatively—two to three children	Opportunities to tell stories
Tends to get out of bounds easily	or play out stories
Enjoys songs and different types of music	Games letting him make
Likes games	some of the rules
Interested in nature activities	Nature materials

FIVE YEARS

Skills	*Play Materials/Activities*
Good motor control, hops, skips, climbs, balances	Climbing, sliding, swinging activities
Explores outside the home	Books that stimulate
Concepts of time, space, number increase	thinking

Can describe pictures with ease
Dresses and undresses alone
Can comply readily with normal requests
Plays imaginatively
Solves most problems
Sings freely
Group play—two to four children
Uses language freely; expresses thoughts freely
Talks without infantile articulation
Likes transportation items
Builds complete structures
Can print a few letters (name)
Can tell a story
Shows pride in accomplishments
Knows most colors
Makes associations
Asks comprehensive questions
Capable of using table manners

Blocks—various sizes—in order on shelves
Art materials (easel painting, clay, water, pencils, crayons, brushes, sand)
Games (simple rules)
Homeliving materials (dolls, dress-up clothes, mirror, and other accessories)
Tricycles
Pictures
Nature materials (animals, fish, insects, pets, plants)
Songs, recordings, sound and rhythm materials
Puzzles (varying levels)
Transportation toys (large and small)
Stories
Games
Excursions

Small- and large-group activities

When planning small-group activities, keep in mind the goals and objectives for the entire hour. Small-group activities should support the learning experiences planned for the large group. Singing is the primary musical activity of a preschool choir. Each small- and large-group activity should include singing as a part of the learning experience. Singing causes children to be consciously involved with the activity because of the response required. Whether the activity involves echoing high and low pitches or discovering fast and slow sounds by changing the tempo of a song, the involvement of the singing voice gives the child an opportunity to display his understanding of the activity.

Knowing the appropriate activities for the preschoolers in your choir requires knowing each preschooler—how he learns; choir instills the feeling that church is a happy place with peo-

his home environment; how he is developing emotionally, spiritually, physically; and his attitude toward music and the church. Knowledge of skills and understandings attainable by preschoolers is also helpful. Study the charts on pages 214-218 to see the sequence in which each musical skill is developed. If an activity is too difficult for your preschoolers, simplify the activity. Should an activity be too simple for your preschoolers, look ahead on the chart for the next level of ability that can be expected. To help make this clear, consider the list of appropriate musical goals for fours and fives.

Through *listening*, preschoolers become aware of sound and silence and different kinds of sounds; identify pitches that are the same or different, high or low, move up, down, or stay the same; identify fast or slow and loud or soft; experience a variety of moods in music; experience music accompanied by instruments or other voices; and experience hymn tunes.

Through *moving*, preschoolers respond to and experience steady beat; sound and silence; rhythm of the words (long and short); sounds that are the same or different; and sounds that move up, down, or stay the same, are high or low, fast or slow, or express a variety of moods.

Through *singing*, preschoolers find the singing voice through making up singing conversations, playing singing games, singing folk songs, singing hymn fragments, and singing accompanied and unaccompanied songs; become aware of good posture and experience songs that contain same and different melodies, express a variety of moods, and contain melodies with high and low pitches and fast and slow tempos.

Through *playing instruments*, preschoolers experience sounds that are the same or different, move up or down or stay the same, are high or low, are fast or slow, and express a variety of moods; become aware of same and different phrases and music accompanied by a variety of instruments.

The *child* is at the center of all planning and preparation. This perspective of preschool choir makes you first a teacher of children and, second, a teacher of music. All the wonderful musical experiences are opportunities to help meet the physical, spiritual, emotional, and social needs of your preschoolers.

A fun movement activity experienced by preschoolers during

ple that care for them and provides the freedom their physical bodies need. The rapid growth periods of preschoolers keep them on the verge of feeling out of control of their ever new and ever larger bodies. Music soothes and calms the restless spirit. Music also is ordered and organized by rhythmic pulses and can help pace the rapidly changing preschoolers through physical activity without their losing control.

Musical activities allow preschoolers opportunities to express spiritual needs. They involve young children in experiences of worship and praise. The awakening spiritual awareness often finds first expression through the singing experiences in preschool choir.

Many emotional needs of preschoolers can be met in the musical environment by loving and caring leaders. *What* you say is not as important as what you *are*. Love is communicated through your attitudes. Preschoolers learn through imitating people before they learn from reading books.

Music helps meet the social needs of preschoolers. Learning to cooperate with other preschoolers is necessary in making music together. This corporate learning can occur in the form of a rhythm activity with nonpitched percussion instruments, in a shared listening/movement activity, and in group involvement in singing a fun song or playing a singing game.

Preschoolers will learn to love music if the leader loves music and helps them develop an appreciation for all types of music. Consider Luke 6:40 (NASB): "A pupil is not above his teacher; but everyone, after he has been fully trained, will be like his teacher."[12]

This Scripture helps us understand the responsibility of leaders. When we recognize that preschoolers (pupils) become like us, *then* the responsibility of the leadership role becomes truly great.

Summary

The prayerful acceptance of the responsibility for leading a preschool choir is the first and most significant step in becoming an effective leader. Your personal commitment will be tested in several areas: attendance, training, the learning environment, integrity, and your consideration for the child.

The room used for making music with fours and fives impacts the learning that takes place. The responses that a room invokes in both leaders and learners affects learning. Usually, the same space used by other preschool organizations of the church is the most appropriate space for preschool choir.

Knowing the appropriate activities for the preschoolers in your choir requires knowing each preschooler—how he learns; his home environment; how he is developing emotionally, spiritually, and physically; and his attitude toward music and the church. Knowledge of skills and understandings that have proven to be attainable by preschoolers is also helpful.

Preschoolers learn through the five senses: hearing, touching, tasting, smelling, and seeing. Of the five senses, hearing, touching, and seeing play the lead roles in the music-learning process.[13] Learning occurs when preschoolers are able to internalize, or gain ownership, of the external experiences in which they participate.

What you say is not as important as what you *are*. Preschoolers learn from imitating people before they learn from reading books.

[1]Charles Businaro, "Selecting Colors for Your Church Facilities," *The Quarterly Review,* April-June 1987, 42.

[2]Ibid., 43-44.

[3]Ibid., 47.

[4]Faber Birren, *Color & Human Response* (New York: Van Nostrand Reinhold Company, 1978), 51. Used by permission.

[5]"Blue Is Beautiful," *Time,* 17 September 1973, 66.

[6]Businaro, "Selecting Colors," 46.

[7]Based on material from Betty Bedsole, Derrell Billingsley, and G. Ronald Jackson, *Leading Preschool Choirs* (Nashville: Convention Press, 1985), 33-36.

[8]Bedsole, Billingsley, Jackson, *Preschool Choirs,* 17.

[9]Ibid.

[10]C. Sybil Waldrop, *Understanding Today's Preschoolers* (Nashville: Convention Press, 1982), 87.

[11]Ibid., 90-92.

[12]From the *New American Standard Bible.* © The Lockman Foundation, 1960, 1962, 1963, 1968, 1971, 1972, 1973, 1975, 1977. Used by permission.

[13]Bedsole, Billingsley, Jackson, *Preschool Choirs,* 17.

*Available from Baptist Book Stores or by calling toll free 1-800-458-BSSB.

**Available from the Customer Service Center, 127 Ninth Avenue, North, Nashville, Tennessee 37234, or by calling toll free 1-800-458-BSSB.

16

How Fours and Fives Respond to Music

Preschoolers learn about music by making music. They learn through *doing*—by developing their musical skills. What they understand about making music—the results of their experiences—become their musical concepts. Preschoolers increase their understanding by adding new ideas to what they have learned through previous experiences. They cannot learn to sing beautifully unless they experience singing. Children must be provided with experiences that help them understand what singing *is* before they can form an understanding (concept) about singing beautifully.

All activities should have relationship to singing in preschool choir.

Listening is the first skill to be developed, for all other skills are dependent on listening. *Moving* is the preschoolers' natural response to music. Through *listening* and *movement* experiences, preschoolers develop concepts about *singing* that will help them to understand how to sing and to develop skill in singing. Helping preschoolers discover their singing voices also will lead to experiences in *playing instruments*. Preschoolers should experience unaccompanied and accompanied singing, using pitched and nonpitched instruments.

Listening

Learning begins with listening. Preschoolers often hear leaders say "Listen to me." They are told to be quiet and listen. What does *quiet* mean? What does *listen* mean? What does *hear* mean? In *Leading Preschool Choirs*, the following distinction is made between *listening* and *hearing*. "Listening is more than just hearing. Hearing is a physiological process, but listening is conscious awareness with a mental response to what is heard. Listening involves the mind. The preschooler who learns to listen soon begins to listen to learn."[1]

Unless preschoolers experience what happens when they listen to sounds they hear with their ears, *listen* will remain a meaningless word to them. Unless preschoolers are given opportunities to experience sounds, compare loud and soft sounds, and experience the accompanying sensations, they will not understand. The admonition, "Listen to me," will be heard, but not understood.

Help preschoolers *see* how they hear. Borrow a model of an ear from a neighborhood science teacher or buy one from a teaching supplies store. Use the model to show the preschoolers how an ear functions. Then help them understand the difference between hearing with their ears and listening with their minds.

Listening Activity #1: Sound or No Sound Game
Purpose: *To discover how to listen.*

This activity requires a room with an observation window; your church nursery may have such a room. Divide the preschoolers into two groups, having one group stay in the room to make sounds while the other group watches through the observation window. When the first group sings a well-known song or plays single percussion instruments, the second group will be able to see sounds being made but will not be able to hear them. Let the groups exchange places and repeat the activity. This concrete experience of sound and no sound will help the preschoolers develop understanding about listening.

Listening Activity #2: Headphone Fun
Purpose: *To discover how to listen.*

Using headphones that will adjust to a preschooler's head, let them take turns wearing the headphones while two or three others sing a well-known song or play instruments. If you do not have headphones, improvise with earmuffs or earplugs. Make sure the preschoolers with the headphones can see the children singing and that all the preschoolers get a turn.

Explain that God gave us ears to hear and encourage the preschoolers to think about what they hear.

Sing "God Gave Me Eyes," repeating stanza 3 several times, changing the words about what preschoolers can hear each time.

God Gave Me Eyes

1. Blue,	blue	sky,	Oh,	I	can	see	the	sky.
2. Red,	red	rose,	Oh,	I	can	smell	a	rose.
3. Ding,	dong,	bell,	Oh,	I	can	hear	a	bell.
4. Yum,	yum,	yum,	Oh,	I	can	taste	ice	cream.
5. Mew,	mew,	mew,	My	kit-ty's	fur	is		soft.

God	gave me	eyes	So	I	can	see	the	sky.
God	gave a	nose	So	I	can	smell	a	rose.
God	gave me	ears	So	I	can	hear	a	bell.
God	gave a	tongue	So	I	can	taste	ice	cream.
God	gave me	hands	So	I	can	feel	how	soft.

From *Nursery Songs and Rhythms* by Margaret L. Crain. Judson Press.

Preschoolers learn through imitation. Show children that you know how to listen by carefully listening to them. Let your responses communicate that you listen when they sing or speak.

Listening Activity #3: Speak and Sing into the Tape Recorder
Purpose: *To discover the difference between the singing voice and the speaking voice.*

Cassette recorders are intriguing to preschoolers. Use this natural curiosity to create a teachable moment. Take a cassette recorder to a small-group area and invite three or four preschoolers to join you. Show them how the recorder works. Allow them to experiment recording their voices and listening to the playback. When all have had a turn, read a short story from *Music Time,*** a poem, or a Bible verse into the tape recorder. Tell the preschoolers they are going to hear your speaking voice when they listen to the recording. Continue the activity by singing a well-known song into the tape recorder. Tell the preschoolers they will hear your singing voice when they listen to the recording. "I Should, Too" is an excellent song to use for this activity.

I Should, Too

Record the preschoolers as they sing this song or a song of your choosing. Record them as they speak the words of the same song. Play the recording and listen to both the speaking voices and the singing voices. Ask the preschoolers to show you how their speaking and singing voices sound differently. In the weeks that follow, plan to bring in recordings of both speaking voices and singing voices that the preschoolers will have not heard previously. Story-telling recordings are excellent sources of speaking voices and *Preschool Music Recording*** or *Preschool Music Cassette*** are good sources for singing voices. Play the recordings and let the preschoolers decide which kind of voices—singing or speaking—they hear.

Through age three, most music listening activities are at the awareness level only. Younger preschoolers respond to music that is loud and soft and fast and slow. The maturing four- and five-year-olds are learning to listen to and understand simple directions given through music. For instance, when they hear "Tap, tap, tap your toes," three-year-olds may or may not tap their toes. Three-year-olds may not know what the word *tap* means, and we should not expect them to know. By age four we can expect preschoolers to know what the word *tap* means or at least to follow our directions after being shown what tapping toes means. Fours should be able to listen to instructions on a recording or in a song and discern the action required.

Listening to learn is a natural progression that follows learning to listen. As preschoolers develop and refine their listening skills, they can demonstrate their understanding of music moving faster or slower by taking any number of actions. They can:

• Move their whole body around the room (locomotor movement).

• Move their arms, hands, or feet as they stay in one place (axial movement).

• Use a manipulative (scarf or ball) as they respond to the music.

Fours are capable of responding to the steady beat when given enough time to securely establish the beat. They can respond to music that changes distinctly and abruptly from fast to slow or slow to fast. The changes in tempo should be obvious. Fours should not be expected to respond as quickly to changes in tempo as fives. As preschoolers grow and develop more muscle control and as the listening skills become better defined, they will be able to respond to more subtle changes and differences, such as obvious phrase changes.

Give your preschoolers many opportunities to experience listening and movement activities. Experiencing is *doing,* and *doing* is how they learn. New skills are developed and mastered through repetition.

Moving

Preschoolers are going to move, so use that natural characteristic constructively. Plan to use movement activities to create many teachable moments. Allow some free movement activities but be ready to demonstrate the responses you want the preschoolers to learn. Preschoolers learn by imitation. If you sing about the action of an animal, show the preschooler how that animal moves.

Movement activities allow the preschoolers some acceptable ways of releasing energy. Show them the kinds of movement responses that are acceptable in the choir setting. Directed movement allows preschoolers to learn to function in a group. The directed movement in singing games fosters an understanding of working together while allowing preschoolers an opportunity to move.

Moving and Listening Activity #1: Ribbons, Scarves, and Wands
Purpose: *To have fun using a manipulative while responding to music.*

Provide a colorful, lightweight ribbon, scarf, or wand (crepe paper fastened to craft stick) for each preschooler. Determine the goal for this listening and movement activity. Will the preschoolers respond to the steady beat, loud and soft, or fast and slow? Choose appropriate music and practice the movements you will demonstrate for the preschoolers. Time the duration of the activity and try to anticipate how physically tiring the activity will be for them. The following recordings have appropriate

movement activities for fours and fives and are available from
Baptist Book Stores.

Everyday Rhythms for Children *
Moving Here and There *
Walk in a Circle *
Hymns for Quiet Times *
Music for Quiet Times *
Sounds of Praise *
Music Is Fun *
Music for Today's Children (Recording Vols. 1, 2, 3) *
Sing a Happy Song *
More Songs for 4's and 5's *
Songs for the Young Child (Cassettes 1 and 2) *
Easy Songs for Early Singers

Moving and Listening Activity #2: Ankle Jingle Bells
Purpose: *To have fun moving to the steady beat.*

Purchase several yards of red or green ribbon and sleigh
bells or jingle bells. Cut the ribbon into eight-inch lengths.
Thread the ribbon through three or four small sleigh bells or
jingle bells and tie the ribbon around the preschoolers' ankles.
Select appropriate seasonal music, such as "Variations on Jingle Bells" from *Everyday Rhythms for Children* and demonstrate marching to the steady beat.
Encourage the preschoolers to march
with you, making the jingle bells ring on
the steady beat. Change the colors of the
ribbons to red, white, and blue and use
with a patriotic recording. Change the colors of the ribbons to blue for raindrop activities.

Moving and Listening Activity #3: Walk, Hop, Tap, Skip, or
Run

Purpose: *To practice steady beat.*

Prepare 15 or 20 three-by-five-inch cards. On each card tape
or glue a picture of preschoolers doing one of the suggested
movement activities: walking, hopping, tapping, skipping, or
running. *Music Time* is a good source for such pictures. If you
cannot find pictures, write these words on the cards: *Walk,*

Hop, Tap, Skip, Run. Place the cards facedown in a stack. Draw a circle, divided into three segments, on a sheet of construction paper. Cut out an arrow and attach it to the center of the circle with a brass fastener. Write one of the following sentences in each section.

Sing a favorite song while you move.
Listen to a recording while you move.
Listen to your leader play a drum while you move.

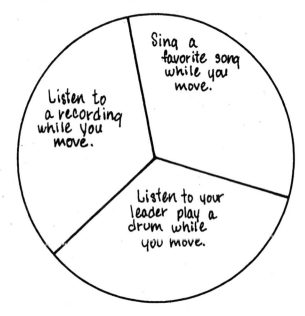

Select a preschooler to choose a card from the stack to tell the group how to move. Select another preschooler to spin the arrow. When the arrow stops, have the preschoolers follow the directions. Continue the activity as long as interest holds.

Moving and Listening Activity #4: Mark the Beat
Purpose: *To visualize the steady beat by marking lines on paper.*

Give each preschooler a crayon or marking pen, a sheet of unlined paper, and a sheet of extra-wide lined paper. Select an appropriate recording from the list in Activity #1 or use a selection from a *Preschool Music Cassette* or *Preschool Music Recording* that has a pronounced steady beat in meter. Demonstrate how to mark the beats on the paper. Show the children how to make a mark for each steady beat; then show them how to arrange the marks in groups of four on the lined paper. Allow plenty of time to practice this activity. See the following diagram.

EXTENSION: Do the activity with older preschoolers as described, using paint and paintbrushes instead of crayons or marking pens.

Preschoolers love activities that involve moving and singing. These are often referred to as singing games. *Sing and Move,* * by Derrell Billingsley, is an excellent resource. When introducing a new singing game, be prepared to sing the song alone until the preschoolers master the movements. After they feel confident in the movements, they may sing and move with you. Since preschoolers usually concentrate on one thought at a time, they may not sing and move at the same time. Specific helps that indicate which songs are best suited to teach steady beat, tone matching, fast or slow, and high or low are given in the index of *Sing and Move.*

Another excellent source of singing games is *Stepping Stones to Matching Tones.* * Creative and helpful suggestions are given with each song.

Singing

Preschoolers delight in singing. Encourage them to develop an even greater enthusiasm for singing by making singing fun. Preschoolers love to sing songs they know. Let this knowledge guide your selection of songs. They need to learn new songs too, however. Choosing songs in a variety of styles will give preschoolers a well-rounded music education. They need to learn the folk songs of their culture, fun songs for their enjoyment, and hymns and Scripture songs for their worship.

Discovering the Singing Voice—Preschoolers find songs more enjoyable after they discover their singing voice. They also find singing more enjoyable, for singing is personal involvement in music making. As long as preschoolers only listen, they are not involved in making music. Help them move from the spectator role to participator. Helping preschoolers find their singing voices and gain confidence in singing is an ambitious goal. Four-year-olds need special help in understanding the difference between singing and speaking. Use their listening and movement skills to help them understand the difference between singing and speaking. Visuals will help preschoolers see and understand the difference between singing and speaking.

Singing Activity #1: Name the Different Types of Voices

Purpose: *To use the speaking, singing, whispering, and shouting voices.*

Introduce the activity with a story you make up about a fire engine hurrying to a fire. Prepare visuals that depict the parts of the story to which the preschoolers can respond. Use pictures of a fire truck rushing to a fire, a building engulfed in flames, firemen holding hoses with water pouring out, a news reporter holding a microphone, and a tired fireman riding on the fire truck.

Tell the preschoolers that when you give a signal with a bell, they are to make the sound of the siren as the fire truck rushes through traffic. Give the preschoolers several opportunities to respond to the bell. Choose two or three preschoolers to perform the actions of the firemen. When the fire truck arrives at the fire, say, "The firemen heard the sizzling and crackling of the fire." Signal the preschoolers to make sounds like a fire burning. Tell them that the firemen jumped from the fire truck and turned on the water to put out the fire. Give the preschoolers a signal to make a sound like water rushing from a hose.

Extend the story to include all sides of the burning building so the preschoolers will have more opportunities to use their shouting voices. Pretend to be a news reporter interviewing the

firemen after the fire was put out. Ask several preschoolers specific questions about the fire. Give as many preschoolers an
opportunity to talk to the reporter as their interest allows. Encourage them to use their best speaking voice for the television
audience. Say: "When the reporter left, the firemen got on their
fire truck and went back to the fire station. On the way back,
the firemen sang this song:

Fire, Fire, Gone Away

Fire, fire, gone a-way, We worked ver-y hard to-day,

Now the fire-men want to play. Fire, fire, stay a-way.

Words by BARBARA SANDERS. Music Traditional.

Encourage the preschoolers to sing the song.

When the story is finished, talk with the preschoolers about
all the different sounds they made during the story. Help them
identify each sound as using the speaking, singing, shouting,
or whispering voice.

Singing Activity #2: Identify the Nonsinging Voices
Purpose: *To use the shouting, whispering, and speaking
voices.*

Set up role-playing situations for the preschoolers that will
give them opportunities to use three voices. Choose preschoolers to role-play the following: a mother, a father, an older sister,
and a preschooler. The remaining preschoolers can be the
crowd at a ball game. Use the following situation.

Tell the children to pretend they are riding in a car with their
parents on their way to see their older sister play a softball
game. Tell them to talk with their parents about how much fun
they will have at the ball game. Encourage them to pretend to
talk about the weather, something they see through the car

window, or where they will go for supper after the game. Tell them to use their normal speaking voices.

When they arrive at the game, talk about cheering for the home run, the man selling hot dogs, or the good play made by the sister. Tell them that this is when they use their shouting voices. (Do not continue this part of the activity as long as the first part. A small amount of the shouting voice will be enough to give contrast.)

When the ball game is over, suggest that the family go for a pizza. Tell them that while they are eating their pizza, they are talking about what happened to each family member during the day. They are talking in a normal voice.

When the family gets into the car to go home, the pre-schooler is very tired and falls asleep. The parents and sister use their soft voices so they will not wake the preschooler.

Singing Activity #3: Contrast Singing and Speaking
Purpose: *To use the speaking voice in response to a specific movement and the singing voice in response to a different type of movement.*

Give the preschoolers two three-inch red circles cut from construction paper and one three-foot length of ribbon or yarn. Place the two red circles on the floor in front of each pre-schooler and lay the ribbon across their knees. Chant "Rain, Rain, Go Away" while alternately tapping on the red circles with the right hand.

Rain, rain, go away,
Come again some other day;
Little Johnny wants to play,
Rain, rain, go away.

Traditional

Next, pick up the yarn or ribbon with the right hand and pull it through the fingers with the left hand while singing "Rain, Rain, Go Away." Talk to the preschoolers about feeling the ribbon slide through the hand while they sing.

Singing Activity #4: Visual Representation of Speaking Voice and Singing Voice

Purpose: *To discover how differently the singing voice feels and sounds from the speaking voice.*

Use red construction paper circles or other shapes to indicate the speaking voice and long strips of blue construction paper to indicate the singing voice. Make the blue strips long enough to indicate phrases in a song you choose. Use enough red circles to indicate each syllable of "Rain, Rain, Go Away."

Place the circles or other shapes on the floor, table, bulletin

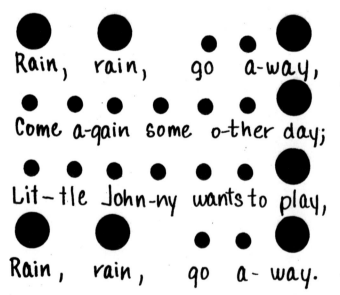

Rain, rain, go a-way,

Come a-gain some o-ther day;

Lit-tle John-ny wants to play,

Rain, rain, go a-way.

Traditional

board, or poster. Point to each shape as you demonstrate how to speak a chant, using one shape for each syllable. Allow the preschoolers to take turns speaking and pointing to the shapes.

Align four of the blue ribbons to a bulletin board or poster board in four rows to represent the four phrases of "Rain, Rain, Go Away." Sing the song while moving your right index finger slowly across the ribbons to indicate a phrase. Tell the preschoolers that you will take a breath at the end of each ribbon. Demonstrate the entire song. Allow the preschoolers to take turns doing the activity.

Singing Activity #5: Role-play "Teddy Bear"
Purpose: *To discover the singing voice while focusing on a game or acting role.*

Sing "Teddy Bear" from *Stepping Stones to Matching Tones* until the preschoolers are confident of the words and melody. Let all the preschoolers pretend to be teddy bears, or choose one preschooler at a time to be the teddy bear. Lead the preschoolers in acting out the words while singing the song. Role playing and pretending are naturally easy for young children to do. Sometimes when playing a role, preschoolers find their singing voices when they have been unable to do so previously. The singing voice often appears when attention is focused on the acting and not on the singing.

Singing Activity #6: Role-play, Using Puppets
Purpose: *To discover the singing voice while focusing on a puppet.*

Make or buy a teddy bear hand puppet. Allow the pre-schoolers to take turns learn-ing to use the puppet. Demonstrate how to use the puppet while singing "Teddy Bear." Let one preschooler work the puppet and sing while the other preschoolers act out what the puppet is sing-ing. Encourage the preschool-ers to make up new actions for the song.

Sometimes a preschooler will be unable to find the singing voice or match pitch until you put a puppet on his hand. When the puppet starts to sing, that voice hidden inside the pre-schooler often appears. Preschoolers may be able to sing while using a puppet and still not be able to sing without the puppet. They may be able to match pitch while pretending to use the puppet's voice even though they have not been able to match pitch before. Some preschoolers can match pitch but do not always choose to do so.

Help preschoolers develop pitch confidence by singing songs they know. Sing a familiar melodic line, using new words. Use *sol* and *mi* to make up songs about whatever you are doing. Make a list of all the *sol-mi* songs you will use for the year. Make another list of *sol-mi-la* songs. Include these favorites from *Stepping Stones to Matching Tones:*

Sol-mi songs:
    Engine, Engine, Number Nine
    God Cares for You
    Hey, Ho, 'Round We Go
    In and Out
    One, Two, Tie My Shoe
    Rain, Rain, Go Away
    The First Name Game

Sol-mi-la songs:
  A Tisket, a Tasket
  Bell Horses
  Bye, Baby Bunting
  Sing unto the Lord a New Song
  Star Light, Star Bright

Other folk song sources contain *sol-mi* and *sol-mi-la* songs for your song file. Consider introducing these to the preschoolers:
  Lemonade
  Snail, Snail
  Bounce High
  Lucy Locket
  Oliver Twist
  Doggie, Doggie
  Cuckoo
  Bee, Bee
  Good Night
  Little Sally Water

Singing Activity #7: Create a New Song on a Known Rhythm Pattern
Purpose: *To create a song on a known rhythmic pattern and identify the melodic rhythm and melody.*
  Review "Hot Cross Buns" (page 31, *Stepping Stones to Matching Tones)* with the preschoolers. Sing and *patsch* the rhythm of the words. Choose one preschooler to play the rhythm of the words (melodic rhythm) on a drum while the

other preschoolers *patsch* the rhythm of the words as they sing. Create new words to the song.

Once preschoolers learn to use their singing voices, use pitch-matching games to help them develop pitch confidence. Have the preschooler sing a pitch; then match the preschooler's pitch. Tape record the activity; take plenty of time to listen to the result.

If a preschooler cannot match pitch, it may be because he is trying too hard. Have the preschooler sing a pitch, and you match his pitch. Record the activity; the preschooler can concentrate on listening to the pitch-matching process as he listens to the tape. Eventually listening and matching pitch will occur at the same time.

Ask the preschoolers to make a siren sound while you record the siren. Play back the tape and let them hear the recorded sound. Play it back again and demonstrate how to match the pitch of the recorded siren. Encourage preschoolers who appear willing to try to match the recorded sound. The listening skill must be developed before pitch matching can make much progress. Once preschoolers are aware of the sensations involved in changing the pitches of the singing and the speaking voices, they can learn to match pitch.

Sing melodies often enough for them to become part of the preschoolers' musical vocabulary. Children need to feel comfortable in knowing a song before they try to match pitch. Four-year-olds do not bring a large repertoire of familiar songs with them from music activities for threes. Strive to develop a core of songs that fours know and identify as theirs. Help fours increase their list of familiar songs to include those they will need when moving on to the five-year-old level. Helping preschoolers increase their repertoire of familiar songs facilitates their development of more accurate singing skills.

Teach four- and five-year-olds a few songs that they can know well rather than many songs that they will never master. The choices should include folk songs, fun songs, game songs, spiritual songs, and some hymn fragments or refrains. Choose refrains within a limited range, such as "Oh, How I Love Jesus," "Jesus Loves Me," "O Come, All Ye Faithful," and others from the list on page 37. A list, such as the one in this book, provides ample song material for both fours and fives. Fours need to learn a group of songs prior to five-year choir, and fives need to learn more songs to take with them to younger children's choir.

Singing Activity #8: Learn a Fun Song
Purpose: *To increase the number of familiar songs.*
Sing "Walk in a Circle." On stanza 3, encourage preschoolers to make up other actions to do. Continue singing the song as many times as there are different actions suggested. Sing stanza 4 between each new action. Keep a list of the actions suggested and count the number of ways they suggested. One suggestion for a new action is:

Now stand still and wiggle your nose,
Now stand still and wiggle your nose,
Now stand still and wiggle your nose,
Wiggle your nose now, children.

Walk in a Circle

1. Walk in a cir-cle, 'round we go,
   Walk in a cir-cle, don't be slow,
   'round we go.
   Walk all a-round, my chil-dren.

2. Walk to the mid-dle, hold hands high,
   Walk to the mid-dle, bye and bye.
   where we were,
   Back to the cir-cle, chil-dren.

3 Now stand still and clap your hands,
   Now stand still and clap your hands.
   clap your hands,
   Stand still and clap now, chil-dren.

4. Walk in a cir-cle, 'round we go,
   Walk in a cir-cle, don't be slow,
   'round we go.
   Walk all a-round, my chil-dren.

Selecting Songs for Fours and Fives—Choose spiritual songs carefully. Select a few songs that reinforce and help teach the spiritual understandings that preschoolers need to develop. Often, too many new songs are introduced. Use and reuse songs so they become a part of the preschoolers to the point that they can sing the songs without thinking. Teach new songs, but give preschoolers many opportunities for repetition so that the new songs become a part of their group of familiar songs. Preschoolers love to repeat songs, probably more so than their leaders. They love to sing songs they know. Leaders can help preschoolers become secure singers by using songs again and again.

Be patient in teaching new songs to preschoolers. Give them time to enjoy each new melody and rhythm pattern. Select five or six songs that four-year-olds can sing throughout the year. Choose these songs with a great deal of care, making sure that the songs are within the appropriate melodic range.

Consider the following list of songs as an appropriate model for a year. Repeat these songs throughout the year. Use this list to help you plan for the entire year.

1. "I Should, Too" (page 6, *I Can Sing!*)
   Spiritual Concepts: God made us.

                        God loves us.

                        God made us special.

                        We should love other people.

2. "God Made a Wonderful World" (page 23, *I Can Sing!*; page 17, *Sing a Happy Song*)
   Spiritual concept: God made everything.

                       God wants us to care for the things He made.

3. "Jesus Loves Children" (page 99, *Music for Today's Children*)
   Spiritual Concept: Jesus loves everyone.

                       I am important to God.

4. "Jesus Is God's Son" (page 8, *I Like to Sing About Jesus*)
   Spiritual Concept: Jesus is God's Son.

                       Jesus loves me.

                       God loves me.

                       I love God and Jesus.

5. "Oh, How I Love Jesus" (page 38, *More Songs for 4's and 5's**)
   Spiritual Concept: I love Jesus.

   Jesus wants people to love Him.

   People sing hymns together at church.

6. "We Can Sing Our Praise to God" (page 9, *I Can Sing!*)
   Spiritual Concept: Singing is a way to praise God.

   Church is a happy place to go.

When you receive *The Music Leader*** each quarter, select the songs from each unit that best fit the needs of your group. If one of the songs from your core list appears as a unit song, it will simply reinforce your goals. If you need to substitute a song from a unit in *The Music Leader* with one from your list, do it. Remember: teaching fours a few songs that they can learn well is better than exposing them to a large number of songs that they will never master.

Different approaches can be used with fives that are not appropriate for fours. At the beginning of the choir year, fives are barely beyond four-year-olds, but you will notice more maturity in fives, especially after January, due to experiences in kindergarten. They are eager learners and are able to retain more material than four-year-olds.

For an excellent description of fours and fives, see *Understanding Today's Preschoolers.** It includes a comparison of the physical, mental, social-emotional, and moral-spiritual development of fours and fives, showing the differences between the two ages.

Discovering the Breath—Breathing is an important part of singing. Preschoolers need experiences that make them aware of their breathing, *but they do not need to understand any of the technical aspects of correct breathing for singing.* Singing Activities 9-11 will help preschoolers develop an awareness of their breath and a readiness for future learning.

Singing Activity #9: Blowing Bubbles for Fun and Breath Support
Purpose: *To become aware of the breath.*

Provide a glass of juice or water and a straw for each preschooler. Demonstrate how to blow bubbles in the water with the straw. Instruct the preschoolers to blow slowly and make the bubbles last as long as possible on one breath. Some preschoolers will try to take a breath and start over. Guide them to understand the goal. When the game is over, refreshments are in order. Add to the fun by providing cheese and crackers.

Singing Activity #10: Bubble Blowing for Fours and Fives
Purpose: *To become aware of the breath.*
  Provide a heavy soap solution and bubble rings for each preschooler. Demonstrate the activity by blowing as large a bubble as you can blow with one long, steady breath. Demonstrate the difference the breath can make by blowing fast, creating many small bubbles. Allow the preschoolers to enjoy the activity, especially if this is the first time they have played with bubbles in an activity. Make it a game, seeing who can make the largest bubble. Repeat this activity several times during the year; repetition is important to preschoolers.

Singing Activity #11: Pinwheel Breathing
Purpose: *To become aware of the breath.*
  Provide a pinwheel for each child, or use the following diagram and guide the preschoolers in making pinwheels. Provide a square piece of paper and a pencil with an eraser for each preschooler and scissors, a box or paper of pins, and a ruler for each leader.
  Hold the pinwheel about 8 to 10 inches from the mouth and blow gently. See how long you can keep the pinwheel moving on one breath. Demonstrate this so the preschoolers can see how to do it. Remind them to take only one breath. The object is to make them aware that their breath has a beginning and ending point and that their breath controls the action of the pinwheel. More specifically, the purpose is *to become aware of the breath.*
  Give each preschooler three turns and count the number of seconds the pinwheel spins on one breath. Record the best effort for comparison with what they are able to do with the same activity at a later date. Use a bell to help the preschoolers realize when one breath has run out. Otherwise, they will take an-

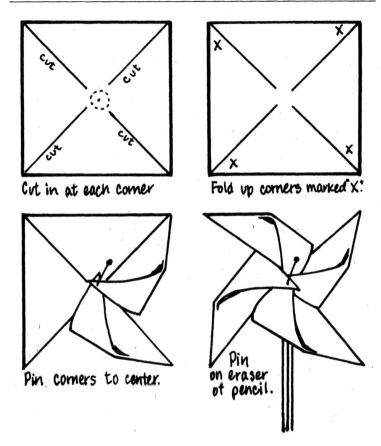

Cut in at each corner

Fold up corners marked "x:"

Pin corners to center.

Pin on eraser of pencil.

other breath and continue blowing without realizing that one breath is over and another one has started.

In his book, *The Diagnosis and Correction of Vocal Faults,* Dr. James C. McKinney states: "The human voice . . . most nearly resembles the brass instruments of the wind family, especially in regard to the actuator. The actuator is the breath of the person. . . . Suggestions borrowed from the technique of various instruments frequently are helpful in solving vocal problems."[4] Acting on Dr. McKinney's statement, provide preschoolers with flutophones and song flutes and let them experiment with blowing into these instruments. The resulting sensation resembles that of singing.

Give the preschoolers a variety of whistles to blow. Use a slide whistle, which produces a whimsical sound and intrigues preschoolers, to make them aware of the breath and its results. Plastic party whistles are inexpensive, and each preschooler can have his own. Use the activity for a small-group learning experience and work with three or four preschoolers at a time. *Becoming Aware of Good Posture*—Posture is an important part of good singing. Model good posture to enable preschoolers to develop an awareness of good singing posture. When choosing specific activities to help preschoolers become more aware of good posture, keep in mind that they only need an awareness. Pace the posture activities with a movement activity that will allow the back muscles to relax. Encourage preschoolers to sit tall when singing. Let them relax between activities. Strive for consistency.

Singing Activity #12: Good Posture Is Tall and Straight
Purpose: *To become aware of good posture.*

Instruct the preschoolers to lie on the floor and curl up in a ball as tightly as they can. Ask them to sing a song from the list in Singing Activity #6. Record their singing. (If you have the capability of videotaping this activity, it will be even more effective.) Next, have them sit on the floor Indian style, lean over, place their elbows on their knees, and sing the same song. Tape record or videotape this version. Record another version with the preschoolers sitting in a chair but leaning forward with their heads between their knees. Finally, record a version with the preschoolers sitting correctly on the edge of their chairs or standing straight while singing the song.

Play back the entire tape with all four versions. Ask the preschoolers to discuss which way sounds best and why. The fourth version should be the best because of the good posture. Be sure to use the same song throughout the activity.

Four-year-olds may laugh because it feels funny to sing all rolled up in a ball. Let them laugh and enjoy the activity. Let them do the activity as many times as they want. Continue the rest of the experiment. Let them hear what making a sound while standing tall feels and sounds like. An important principle to remember during this activity is that children mirror what they see adults doing. Unless adults consistently model good posture in sitting and standing while singing, the activity will be ineffective.

As an ongoing emphasis on personal physical growth, display a measurement chart and record each preschooler's height and weight several times during the year. Remind them to stretch their tallest when measured for height.

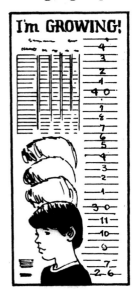

Display the chart in the large-group area so you can refer to it, reminding the preschoolers of good posture. During small group, measure the preschoolers for good singing posture. Accept this as a teachable moment for them to feel the tall stretch of the spine. As each preschooler is measured, lead the group in singing songs about growing, such as "There's No One Exactly Like Me"[0/00] and "Every Day I'm Getting Bigger."[0/00]

Singing Activity #13: Human Posture Puppets
Purpose: *To be more aware of good posture.*
Let the preschoolers pretend to be human puppets. Encourage them to act like a puppet on a string with you controlling the strings to make them very tall. It may even be possible to bring an actual marionette and let the puppet demonstrate examples of singing with good posture. Give the puppet a name like Mr. Forgetful. Have another leader work Mr. Forgetful while he and the preschoolers sing a song together. Let Mr. Forgetful slump lower and lower as he sings. Ask the preschoolers what the puppet needs to do to become a better singer. Let them show Mr. Forgetful how to keep from running out of breath by standing tall and singing "There's No One Exactly Like Me," "Every Day I'm Getting Bigger," or "I Can."[0]

Playing Instruments

Preschoolers become more involved in the learning process when they play instruments. Add a few nonpitched percussion instruments for them to play the steady beat of a favorite song and watch their interest increase. Preschoolers learn from concrete experiences in steady beat, melodic rhythm, same and different patterns, high and low pitches, loud and soft sounds, fast and slow tempos, and expression through playing instruments. Adding to those benefits is the pure pleasure of accompanying a song with instruments. Smiles light up the faces of preschoolers when they discover how to transfer *patsch*ing a steady beat on the knees to playing it on rhythm sticks or a hand drum. Instruments make learning fun.

Teaching preschoolers to play instruments requires planning and preparation. Preschoolers need to experience success. Handing new rhythm instruments to preschoolers and expecting them to play will prove disappointing for them and disastrous for you. Learning to play the various instruments takes time and repetition. Careful preparation and patient demonstration of the use of instruments will bring good results. Allow time for the children to experiment with the sounds of the instruments.

The sound of an Autoharp is fascinating and intriguing. *Using the Autoharp with Preschoolers and Children,* * by Madeline Bridges, contains helpful information about playing and using the Autoharp. Section I provides instruction for the leader to learn how to play the Autoharp. *The Music Leader* often contains activities for the Autoharp.

Preschoolers enjoy playing nonpitched percussion instruments. Demonstrate the acceptable way to play any percussion instrument you give them; then allow time for them to experiment on their own. Instill a respect for musical instruments by insisting that all instruments, including rhythm sticks, be treated carefully and played properly. Preschoolers can have successful experiences with many instruments. In addition to the piano, activities in the curriculum materials *(The Music Leader, Music Time, Preschool Music Resource Kit,* and *Preschool Music Cassette/Preschool Music Recording)* include the following rhythm instruments:

- Step bells
- Autoharp
- Rhythm sticks
- Drum
- Wrist bells
- Claves
- Tone block
- Tambourine
- Triangle
- Finger cymbals
- Sand blocks
- Resonator bells
- Xylophone

Pictures of these rhythm instruments are available in *Classroom Instrument Poster Set.* *

Instruments that produce melodies are interesting to preschoolers. Success with melody instruments is generally considered limited to persons with music-reading ability. Preschoolers, however, can have successful experiences with melody instruments. Older preschoolers can read color-coded charts and learn short melodic phrases by rote. Other preschoolers can play short melodic *ostinati*. Free accompaniment experimentation, using the pentatonic scale, is yet another way for preschoolers to have successful experiences with melody instruments. Pentatonic accompaniments are easy for them to play on the piano because the pentatonic scale may be played on the five black keys.

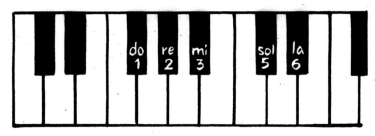

The pride and joy radiating on the preschoolers' faces when playing resonator bells or xylophones is worth the time and effort it takes to prepare activities for them. While bars are available for all the scale pitches, many accompaniment patterns can be played with the C, F, and A bars.

The piano can be used with preschoolers in much the same way as resonator bells and barred instruments. To prepare the piano for musical activities, mark the piano keys with removable, color-coded adhesive dots to make it easy for preschoolers to find the correct notes to play. Allow the children to experiment with loud and soft and long and short sounds at the piano. Activities that use high- and low-sounding pitches are abstract and sometimes more difficult for preschoolers to understand when using a piano. The lateral left-to-right motion creating a low-to-high sound is confusing to preschoolers; they cannot relate horizontal movement of the hands on the keyboard with the vertical low-to-high sounds.

Acquaint the preschoolers with electronic keyboards, which are available in a wide range of prices and variety of styles. Many of the keyboards are small instruments with keys barely wide enough for the fingers of small preschoolers. When considering a keyboard for the preschool choir room, buy one with full-size keys. Use these keyboards as you would a piano and use removable adhesive dots to color code the keys. Electronic keyboards provide intriguing sounds that captivate preschoolers. These sounds are part of today's musical world. Try adding an electronic keyboard to your resources for preschoolers.

Playing Activity #1: A Flyswatter and an Autoharp
Purpose: *To discover a different sound with the Autoharp in a steady beat activity.*

Purchase an inexpensive all-plastic flyswatter. Review a favorite fun song with the preschoolers. As the choir sings the song, let a preschooler swat the strings of the Autoharp with the flyswatter while you press the chord bars. If you select a one-chord song, let a second preschooler press the chord bar. Take photos and use the pictures later at a Parents' Night or display them on a bulletin board.

All the songs in *Stepping Stones to Matching Tones,* pages 5-30, are one-chord songs and may be played with the C major chord. "Zum Gali Gali" is a popular one-chord song to use with preschoolers.

Zum Gali Gali

1. Zum ga-li ga-li ga-li, Zum ga-li ga - li,
2. An - drew can play the Au - to - harp, See him tap - ping.

Zum ga-li ga-li ga-li, Zum ga-li ga - li.
Fly swat-ters are a lot of fun, See him tap - ping.

Palestinian Work Song.

Playing Activity #2: Chopstick Rhythm Sticks
Purpose: *To play a steady beat accompaniment to a song or recording.*

Purchase enough inexpensive chopsticks for each preschooler to have a pair. When struck together, chopsticks make a softer sound than regular rhythm sticks, allowing the preschoolers to hear the music better. Have the preschoolers hold one chopstick in the left hand, palm up, and tap it with another chopstick held in the right hand and play the steady beat to "Variations on Chopsticks" from *Everyday Rhythms for Children* recording. The music for this recording is printed in the book by the same title. Variation I is an experience in $\frac{3}{4}$. Variation II is in $\frac{4}{4}$ and includes a section that gets faster and faster. Variation III is a medium tempo in $\frac{6}{8}$, and the steady beat is marked with accents in the book. Preschoolers will be able to feel the two strong beats of $\frac{6}{8}$ meter.

"Playing the Lummi Sticks," page 20, *Stepping Stones to Matching Tones,* is another good song to which preschoolers may tap a steady beat. Teach the song to the boys and girls several weeks before you ask them to sing and play the steady beat together. Always make adequate preparation for rhythm activities so the preschoolers can have successful experiences.

Playing Activity #3: *Sol-mi* with Resonator Bells
Purpose: *To play a steady beat accompaniment to a* sol-mi *song.*

Select a *sol-mi* song from the list of songs that you plan to use during the year. Choose one preschooler to play the *sol* (G) bell and another to play the *mi* (E) bell. Instruct them to hold

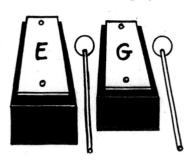

the bell in one hand and the mallet in the other hand and lightly tap the steady beat in the middle of the bell. Lead the rest of the preschoolers in singing the song and *patsch*ing the steady beat on their knees. The *patsch*ing will help the preschoolers who are playing the resonator bells.

Playing Activity #4: Xylophones for Fun
Purpose: *To experience steady beat on the xylophone.*

Use your largest xylophone. The bass xylophone is best for preschoolers. Provide two pairs of felt xylophone mallets. Remove all the bars except the F, A, and C bars. Invite two pre-

schoolers to kneel on the floor, holding the mallets as though they were the handlebars of a tricycle. Demonstrate for the preschoolers how to tap the bar in the middle while holding the mallets loosely. Demonstrate playing any two notes on the steady beat and singing the one-chord song, "Come and Sing with Me." Invite the two preschoolers to play any two notes on the steady beat while you sing and the other preschoolers *patsch* the steady beat. Next, ask the other preschoolers to sing with you. If the two preschoolers playing the xylophone are comfortable both singing and playing, encourage them to do so.

Come and Sing with Me

I like you,   you like me,   Come and *sing with   me;

Hear a song,   *sing a-long,   Come and *sing with   me.

*Substitute: clap, hop, play, move.

Playing Activity #5: Preschoolers at the Piano
Purpose: *To experience a steady beat, using the piano.*

Teach the preschoolers "Hot Cross Buns" from *Songs Every Child Can Play.** Let them sing it for two weeks before adding a piano accompaniment. When they are able to sing it confidently, place three preschoolers in three positions along the piano keyboard: low, middle, and high. Clap a steady beat and ask each of them to play the steady beat with you, each playing the black keys G♭ and D♭. Enlarge the following diagram and make a poster for the preschoolers to see.

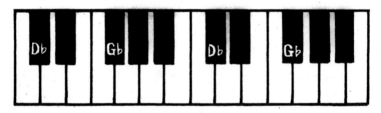

Have the rest of the group *patsch* or clap the steady beat with you. When the steady beat is established, have the children sing the song with you.

EXTENSION: Create new words for "Hot Cross Buns."

Example: Hear us play, hear us play,
Play together, play together,
Hear us play.

Enjoy playing instruments with preschoolers. Successful instrumental experiences are realized through preparation and abundant patience.

Summary

Preschoolers learn about music by making music. They learn through *doing*. Preschoolers increase their understanding by adding new ideas to what they have learned through previous experiences.

Listening is the first skill to be developed, for all other skills are dependent on listening. *Moving* is the preschoolers' natural response to music. Through *listening* and *movement* experiences, preschoolers develop concepts about *singing* that will help them to understand how to sing and to develop skill in singing. Helping preschoolers discover their singing voices will also lead to experiences in *playing instruments*. Preschoolers should experience unaccompanied and accompanied singing, using pitched and nonpitched instruments.

Singing is the most significant activity in preschool choir. Give them plenty of opportunities to *sing*. Be aware of your own good singing habits; remember: fours and fives imitate adults. They choose a role model to emulate. They model what they see you do, what they hear you do, how they see you act, and what they perceive as the way you feel about what you are doing. Even our attitudes are contagious. Preschoolers are always learning; adults are always teaching.

---

[1]Betty Bedsole, Derrell Billingsley, and G. Ronald Jackson, *Leading Preschool Choirs* (Nashville: Convention Press, 1985), 41.

[2]Songs from Eleanor G. Locke, ed., *Sail Away: 155 American Folk Songs to Sing, Read and Play* (New York: Boosey and Hawkes, 1981).

[3]Songs from Lois Choksy, *The Kodály Context: Creating an Environment for Musical Learning* (Englewood Cliffs, NJ: 1981).

[4]James C. McKinney, *The Diagnosis and Correction of Vocal Faults* (Nashville: Broadman Press, 1982), 27.

*Available at Baptist Book Stores or by calling toll free 1-800-458-BSSB.

**Available from the Customer Service Center, 127 Ninth Avenue, North, Nashville, Tennessee 37234 or by calling toll free 1-800-458-BSSB.

0Songs from *More Songs for 4's & 5's*.

00Songs from *Music for Today's Children*.

17

Leading a Preschool Choir
for Fours and Fives

Expectations

According to the Random House *American College Dictionary, expectation* is "anticipation; a thing looked forward to; a prospect of future good."

The director of a preschool choir brings expectations to the leadership role. The director expects the church to provide a place for the choir to meet, literature and equipment to use, and a support system of encouragement and training. The director expects parents' to bring preschoolers to choir, ready to participate. The director expects the preschoolers to be healthy, cooperative, and ready to be loved. The director expects the parents to welcome a home visit from the director. The director expects other choir leaders to be present, punctual, and prepared for choir, and to attend planning meetings and training events.

The church has expectations also. It expects the preschool choir director and leaders to uphold the practices and principles of the church. The church expects all choir activities to point the preschooler toward a personal relationship with Jesus as Savior and Lord and to help the preschooler learn to use music at church and at home. Above all, the church expects the director and leaders to uphold and teach the spiritual truths of the Bible.

Parents have expectations. Parents expect the preschool choir leaders to be ready when their preschoolers arrive. Parents expect their preschoolers to be loved and guided with patience and firmness. They may expect to observe their preschoolers in the choir setting at appropriate times throughout the year. Parents expect their preschoolers to have enjoyable experiences in choir.

The preschoolers themselves have expectations. They expect to be loved unconditionally by their choir leaders. They expect the leaders to remember their names. They expect their fair share of turns in rehearsal activities. They expect to learn new songs and participate in singing; moving, listening, and playing instruments activities. Preschoolers may come to expect many of the songs they learn to be about Jesus, God, and their church. They expect boundaries within which to function. Preschoolers have high expectations, and choir leaders must be ready and willing to meet those expectations.

Decisions

A *decision* is a determination of a question; a judgment, a making up of one's mind. Many decisions must be made about preschool choir. Decisions must be made about the length of rehearsal, the day of rehearsal, and the time of day the choir will meet. A decision must be made concerning where the choir will meet and how to arrange the space. Still other decisions must be made based on the number of preschoolers and leaders, the budget, and the priorities of the church. Some of those decisions may not be made by the choir director or leaders; decisions related to scheduling, the church calendar, and room assignments may be made by the church staff.

The decisions about what to do within parameters of the schedules, calendar, and assigned space are more strongly influenced by the director and leaders. Managing the schedule to the preschoolers' advantage is your challenge. The day of the week when the choir meets has some bearing on how you will plan. The time of day has a tremendous bearing on the types of activities that will work successfully with preschoolers. Special events and emphases also have a strong bearing on how and what you choose to do with your preschoolers. The space assigned affects the types of activities that can be done. Some movement activities may have to be adapted if space is limited. The location and number of electrical outlets will influence the use of record players and other electronic equipment. Heating, cooling, lighting, bathroom facilities, and access to water must be considered when planning activities for your preschoolers.

Directors and leaders should clearly understand all decisions that affect the preschoolers during choir. You are the voice of the preschoolers in the decision process. As you plan, remember that you are a teacher of children first and a teacher of music second. The decisions you make should be made for the ultimate well-being of the preschoolers and to provide an optimum learning environment in which they can have happy music experiences.

Decisions about curriculum materials are usually influenced by the needs and strengths of everyone involved—the director, leaders, preschoolers, and the church. (See chapter 7, "Planning Musical Experiences for Preschoolers," for a description of the curriculum materials.)

Pacing

Pacing is the rate of movement or progression. Pacing is how you move the preschoolers through the sequence of learning. Planning is the backbone of pacing; flexibility is the salvation of pacing. Without adequate planning for preschoolers, you may not realize how long you have them seated, playing the Autoharp or putting together a music puzzle. Preschoolers will move every two or three minutes. If you alternate between movement and nonmovement activities, you will hold the preschoolers' interest, and opportunities for those teachable moments you desire will occur.

Pacing also depends on how the leaders and preschoolers respond to each other. The following suggestions follow the format of the units in *The Music Leader*. Adapt the plans to meet the needs of your preschoolers.

• *Early-arriver Activities*—Starts when the first preschooler arrives; be prepared to begin them as early as 15 minutes before the scheduled starting time. Spend this time becoming better acquainted with individual preschoolers. Early-arriver activities are good opportunities to explore the singing voice. Use activities with the same purpose as those planned for small-group time.

• *Large-group Time (optional)*—About 10 minutes of transitional activities to prepare preschoolers for the remainder of the rehearsal. Use this time to review a favorite well-known song or a new song from the previous session. Use a listening and movement activity to capture the wiggles.

• *Small-group Time*—About 20-25 minutes of activities that relate to the goals of the unit. All activities should relate to the second large-group activity.

• *Large-group Time*—About 20-30 minutes of activities involving the preschoolers together. Pacing is crucial during this time. The challenge to director or leader in charge is to keep all the preschoolers focused on the same activity.

When preschoolers stay too long with one activity, they may continue to do the activity without conscious thought while the mind focuses on another activity. Often, they will go to the activity that has captured their attention. The activity the preschooler chooses for the moment may or may not be compatible with the rest of the learners in the large group. Pace the activities so that each two- or three-minute time segment is different from the preceding two or three minutes. Change from a movement to a nonmovement activity, from fast to slow, listening to singing, loud to quiet, seated to standing, with instruments to without instruments, a favorite song or activity to a new song or activity.

Three consecutive activities that keep the preschoolers seated quietly is an example of poor pacing. The same is true for three movement activities. Variety is important. Change the learning environment by physically changing the large-group area. Change from being seated on the floor to using chairs. Change actual seating position of the children—do not always let the same preschoolers sit by each other. Pacing is controlling the learning environment. Adequate pacing is crucial to happy music experiences for preschoolers.

Pacing also involves the presentation of activities. Use as many methods and techniques as possible to make learning fun. Vary your presentations of new songs and activities by using art, drama, puppetry, rebus charts, and hands-on visual aids. Also, vary your teaching technique. How many ways can a song be taught effectively? Search for the answer to that question, and you will have young singers eager to learn new songs.

Use the following steps in the sample activity when introducing a new skill or understanding (concept):

Step 1—Introduction
Step 2—Demonstration
Step 3—Practice
Step 4—Application/Review

Sample Activity

Purpose: *To sing and move to the steady beat of a song or recording.*

Step 1—Introduction

• Use two or three favorite songs with a pronounced (easily felt) steady beat, such as "I Make Music, Too" (page 93, *More Songs for 4's & 5's**), "Bow, Wow, Wow" (page 39, *Stepping Stones to Matching Tones**), or refrain to "There Is a Name I Love to Hear" (No. 66, *Baptist Hymnal,* 1975) or "Oh, How I Love Jesus" (No. 217, *The Baptist Hymnal*).

• Sing one of the songs for the preschoolers; then teach the song to them by echo singing (a phrase at a time, with the children repeating after you). Spend several sessions carefully teaching the three songs. Use different techniques in presenting the other two songs. Use a rebus (pictures for the concrete words) to teach one of the songs. Use a puppet to teach the third song or let it represent a child and echo sing the song with the puppet. Spend enough time with the songs for all the preschoolers to be successful in their singing, listening, and moving. This is a critical step, for preschoolers learn by adding new knowledge to that which they already know. They need to know several songs well from which to extract new learning.

1. Sing one of the songs from the list and clap the steady beat.

2. Invite preschoolers to sing the song with you. Repeat singing and clapping the song several times (as interest dictates).

3. Tell the preschoolers that all songs have a *steady beat.*

Step 2—Demonstration
1. Relate the new term *steady beat* to something the preschoolers understand, such as a clock ticking or a heart beating. With a stethoscope, let the preschoolers hear their own heartbeats. Ask a child to walk across the room as you match his footsteps with a drumbeat.

2. Ask a child to play a steady beat on a drum as you walk across the room, matching your footsteps to his drumbeat.

3. When a child has trouble feeling the steady beat, clap your hands on his hands to the steady beat of a recording or as you sing a song together.

Step 3—Practice
1. Sing one of the songs without demonstrating the steady beat. Ask the preschoolers to clap the steady beat of this song.

2. Continue letting the preschoolers discover and clap the steady beat in familiar songs.

Step 4—Discovery and Application
1. Continue to experience and identify the steady beat in other songs the preschoolers know and in familiar listening and movement activities. When they are comfortable with the term *steady beat*, use it with every song they sing. Guide the preschoolers in finding the steady beat in every new song.

2. Look and listen for preschoolers not responding to the steady beat.

3. Review Step 2—Demonstration for those not responding to the steady beat.

Management

Management is the act or manner of handling, direction, or control; a skill in managing. The preschool choir director, who is responsible for planning meetings, large-group times, keeping track of equipment and supplies, coordinating with other choirs and other preschool activities at the church, might more correctly be called a manager.

If you do not feel your management skills are adequate, take heart in the knowledge that they can be sharpened with practice. Make yourself a procedures notebook and write out a step-by-step plan of action for every responsibility. Organize your thoughts on paper. It helps to know what to do next and what has not yet been done. Meet your responsibilities systematically by maintaining records, preparing and filing resource kit items, and generally keeping up with all the work that must be done.

You may find it helpful to list the following responsibilities in your notebook; leave space under each item to add personal notes.

1. Contacting absentees
    Who pays for postage and cards?
2. Scheduling special events
    Training sessions
    Parents Night at Choir
3. Securing curriculum materials for each quarter
    When?
    Where?
    How?
4. Using the resource room
    Check-out requirements
    Inventory lists
5. Preparing the room for choir
6. Using the media library
    How to check out equipment
    Inventory lists
7. Preparing and filing issues of *Preschool Music Resource Kit*
8. Refreshments
    How?
    Where?
    When?
9. Responding to emergencies
    Telephone numbers of fire, ambulance, doctors, hospital, and police
    Location of fire escapes
    Procedure for responding to the illness or injury of a child
10. Requesting purchases and reimbursement of funds
    Are purchase order numbers required?
    List of budget numbers

Successful preschool choir directors are usually persons with many other responsibilities related to home, family, work, other church activities, and community activities. The implementation and practice of good management principles and skills help ensure successful musical experiences for your preschoolers and also make directing and leading a preschool choir an enjoyable experience.

Summary

Directors and leaders should clearly understand all decisions that affect the preschoolers in choir. Keep the children in mind as you plan. The decisions you make should be made for the ultimate well-being of all the preschoolers and to provide an optimum learning environment in which they can have happy music experiences.

Pacing is how you move the preschoolers through the sequence of learning. It is the presentation of activities during rehearsal, and it depends on how the leaders and preschoolers respond to each other. Use as many methods and techniques as possible to make learning fun. Planning is the backbone of pacing.

Use the following three steps when introducing a new skill or understanding (concept):

Step 1—Preparation and Practice

Step 2—Identification

Step 3—Discovery and Application

Meet your responsibilities systematically by maintaining records, preparing and filing resource kit items, and keeping up with the nonmusical but necessary work that must be done.

Resources

Resources manifest themselves in many forms. Friends who share a common interest and can discuss activities that relate to the preschool choir are a rich resource. A visit over a cup of coffee can result in a wealth of ideas and techniques for leading preschoolers. Cultivate those friends and cherish them as valuable resources.

Printed materials and equipment are the most common resources. Plan for their proper care in storage and use. The following resources are available to preschool leaders.

Church Literature

  ***Help Your Child to Music*
  **Music Time
  ***Preschool Music Cassette*
  ***Preschool Music Recording*
  ***Preschool Music Resource Kit*
  **The Music Leader

Songbooks

  *More Songs for 4's & 5's
  *Music for Today's Children
  *The Baptist Hymnal

Collections

  *Easy Songs for Early Singers
  *I Can Sing!
  *More Songs for 4's & 5's for the Autoharp, Sets 1 and 2
  *Preschool Songs for the Autoharp
  *Sing a Happy Song
  *Sing and Move
  *Songs for the Young Child

Recordings

  *Activity Songs for Tiny Tots
  *Easy Songs for Early Singers
  *Everyday Rhythms for Children
  *Hymns for Quiet Times
  *I Make Music, Too
  *More Hymns for Quiet Times
  *More Songs for 4's & 5's, Vol. 1, 2, 3, 4
  *Music for Quiet Times
  *Music for Today's Children, Vol. 1, 2, 3
  *Select Songs for Children, Vol. 1, 2, 3
  *Sing a Happy Song
  *Songs for the Young Child, Cassettes 1 and 2
  *Songs for Tiny Tots
  *Sounds of Praise

Guidance

* *ChromAharP Tuning Kit*
* *Classroom Instrument Poster Set*
* *Everyday Rhythms for Children*
* *Games/Playthings Music Teaching Pack*
* *How to Guide Preschoolers*
* *Leading and Accompanying Children's Singing*
* *Musical Experiences for Preschoolers; Birth through Three*
** *Music for Threes*
* *Preschool and Children's Choirs Plan Book*
* *PromoIdeas for Preschool and Children's Choirs*
* *Sing and Move*
* *Singing Games for Children*
* *Stepping Stones to Matching Tones*
* *Teaching Children to Sing*
* *Teaching Music Concepts Through Art Activities*
* *The Choir Coordinator's Notebook*
* *Understanding Today's Preschoolers*
* *Understanding Today's Preschoolers Resource Kit*
* *Using Kodály and Orff in the Church*
* *Using the Autoharp with Preschoolers and Children*

Song List

Hymns or Hymn fragments/refrains

"America, the Beautiful" (last two lines—Key of F)
"Go, Tell It on the Mountain" (refrain)
"His Name Is Wonderful" (first two lines—Key of C)
"Holy Bible, Book Divine" (first two lines—Key of C)
"Jesus Loves Me"
"O Come, All Ye Faithful" (refrain)
"Rejoice, Ye Pure in Heart" (refrain)
"Tell the Good News" (Key of C)
"There Is a Name I Love to Hear" (refrain)

Spiritual Concept Songs

"Christmas Tells of Jesus,"°/°° *Songs for the Young Child*
"God Cares For You,"† *Stepping Stones to Matching Tones*
"God Gave Me Eyes,"° *Songs for the Young Child*

"God Loves Everyone," *I Can Sing!*

"God Made a Wonderful World," *I Can Sing!; Sing a Happy Song*

"I Should, Too," *I Can Sing!*

"Jesus Is God's Son," *I Like to Sing About Jesus*

"Learn of God's Love," *I Like to Sing About Jesus*

"People Praise God"°

"Tell Me That God Loves Me"°

"The Bible Is a Special Book"°/°°

"When I Pray"°/°° *Songs for Children*

Singing Games

"Bow, Wow, Wow," *Stepping Stones to Matching Tones*

"Engine, Engine, Number Nine,"† *Stepping Stones to Matching Tones; Sing and Move*

"London Bridge," *Sing and Move*

"Mulberry Bush," *Music for Today's Children* (Change to key of D)

"Teddy Bear,"† *Stepping Stones to Matching Tones*

Fun Songs

"Autumn Leaves Are Now Falling,"°° *Songs for Children* (Change to key of C)

"Black Cows," *Early Songs for Early Singers*

"Every Day I'm Getting Bigger,"°/°°

"Hi-yi-yi-yi, Yee!," *I Like to Sing About Jesus*

"I Can Be"°°

"Isn't It Fun?,"°° *Songs for the Young Child*

"Listen! Listen!,"† *Easy Songs for Early Singers*

"Pitter, Patter, Pit,"†/° *Songs for the Young Child*

"Pretty Colored Butterfly," *Sing and Move*

"Thanksgiving Day"°/°°

"The Donkey," *The Music Leader* 10/84

"You're a Special Child,"†/†† *Easy Songs for Early Singers*

Music Concept Songs

"A Song Just Comes Out," *The Music Leader* 10/90

"I Can Clap and Sing," *The Music Leader* 1/80, 7/84, 1/87

"I Can Hear the Music," *The Music Leader* 7/84, 4/85

"I Can Sing!," *I Can Sing!*
"I Make Music, Too," *The Music Leader* 1/75, 10/85, 7/87
"Loud or Soft?"††
"Marching"°/°°
"Music Helps Me Talk to God," *The Music Leader* 7/89
"Music Time with Friends,"°°
"My Tambourine,"°°
"We're Making Music Together,"°
"With My Voice," *Sing a Happy Song*

---

*Available at Baptist Book Stores or by calling toll free 1-800-458-BSSB.
**Available from the Customer Service Center, 127 Ninth Avenue, North, Nashville, Tennessee 37234, or by calling toll free 1-800-458-BSSB.
†Songs from *Musical Experiences for Preschoolers; Birth Through Three.*
††Songs from *Music for Threes.*
°Songs from *More Songs for 4's & 5's.*
°°Songs from *Music for Today's Children.*

Glossary

Activity Teaching
Teaching through planned experiences that require the pre-schoolers' active participation. Preschoolers learn by doing rather than being told or shown.

Axial Movement
Movements made while sitting or standing in place (swinging, swaying, rocking, rowing, clapping, *patschen*, and snapping fingers).

Concept
An idea conceived in the mind. An understanding or insight that grows out of experiences.

Early-arriver Activity
An activity which permits early-arriving children to participate immediately without stopping the activity to start over each time a child arrives.

Echo Clap
A technique for teaching in which the leader claps a pattern or phrase and the child or children claps the pattern or phrase in strict imitation.

Echo Sing
A technique for teaching in which the leader sings a pattern or phrase and the child or children sing the pattern or phrase in strict imitation.

Glissando
A rapid sliding up or down the musical scale. On the piano, it involves drawing the thumb or another finger over the keys.

Glockenspiel
A melody instrument with removable bars.

Hand Signs
Visuals for teaching children to sing on pitch. They are made by the hand placed across the front of the body, showing the vertical relationship of scale notes to each other with *do* at waist level and a gradually higher position for each of the following. *La* should be at eye level and *do* above the head. *(See diagram on following page.)*

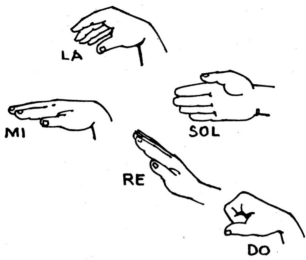

Internalization

The realization of learning, accompanied by confidence gained through mastery of a skill.

Locomotor Movement

Movements made while moving from one place to another (walking, marching, running, tiptoeing, jumping, hopping, skating, and skipping).

Large-Group Activities

Activities done with all the children together—everyone engaged in the same activity such as singing a song, or in closely related activities such as some children singing a song while others play an *ostinato* for the song.

Metallophone

A melody instrument with light alloy metal tone bars. The sustaining quality it makes is appropriate for patterns of half notes and whole notes.

Ostinato

A rhythmic or melodic pattern repeated throughout a song. *Ostinati* is the plural of *ostinato*.

Pacing

The practice of regulating the rhythm and flow of learning experiences based on the mood and interest level of children in a learning environment.

Patsch
· A rhythmic movement made by patting or slapping the thighs with one or both hands.

Pentatonic Scale
A five-tone scale made up of whole steps and minor thirds. *Fa* (fourth scale degree) and *ti* (seventh scale degree) are omitted so that no half steps are present. Example of a pentatonic scale in the key of C: CDEGA.

Preschool Music Activity Group
A music organization for preschoolers from birth through three years old, consisting of learning centers (homeliving, art, blocks, and nature) in which the participating adults' involvement is primarily based on the children's questions and comments.

Preschool Choir
A music organization for four- and five-year-olds consisting of small- and large-group activities in which the participating adults' roles are facilitator and enabler, guiding the children to make discoveries in musical experiences.

Resonator Bells
A melody instrument with individual tone blocks for each tone. The sustaining quality of this instrument makes it appropriate for patterns of half notes and whole notes.

Small-Group Activities
Activities done by groups of two to five preschoolers. Several small groups may function at the same time. Each group may do a different activity or all the small groups may do the same activity.

Steady Beat
The basic underlying beat, or pulsation, in music.

Step Bells
A melody instrument with nonremovable tone bars which are mounted on steps, giving a visual perception of up and down and whole and half steps.

Tempo
The speed at which music is played or sung.

Xylophone
A melody instrument with removable wood bars.

MUSICAL DEVELOPMENT

UNBORN	BIRTH TO THREE MONTHS	THREE TO SIX MONTHS	SIX TO NINE MONTHS	NINE TO TWELVE MONTHS
LISTENING				
Hears and feels music.	Turns toward source of musical sound. Is calmed by music.	Continues to turn toward source of musical sound. Continues to be calmed by music (lullabies).	Continues to turn toward source of musical sound. Discovers that music is more than lullabies. Begins to listen intently.	Begins to show musical preferences.
MOVING (Rhythm)				
Moves when music is played.	Moves in response to musical sound.	Stops moving to turn toward source of musical sound.	Sways or moves up and down after listening intently to music.	Remembers simple motions to nursery songs.
SINGING (Vocalizing, Chanting)				
	Expresses feelings by crying.	Continues to express feelings by crying. Begins to make babbling sounds.	Attempts to make vocal sounds: • that are different from melodies and rhythms heard. • before first attempts to speak.	Tries to imitate vocal sounds and melodies. Cannot match pitches.

TWELVE TO EIGH-TEEN MONTHS	EIGHTEEN TO TWENTY-FOUR MO.	TWO YEARS	THREE YEARS
LISTENING			
Begins to listen to music without being distracted.	Continues to listen to music without distraction. Does not like some music, but will continue to listen for awhile.	Continues to listen to music, but listens for longer periods of time. Becomes aware of: • the rhythm of the words of a song • fast and slow • loud and soft Recognizes a song by the sounds of the words.	Continues to listen attentively to music. Becomes aware of same and different sounds. Responds to: • fast and slow • loud and soft
MOVING (Rhythm)			
Experiences: • large movements to music • varying movements to music • use of space when moving • repetition of some movements Movements are not coordinated with music.	Responds by: • moving to music with others. • moving while singing. • attempting unsuccessfully to coordinate movements to the rhythm of the music.	Responds by: • moving to music less than when a baby. • moving after hearing many repetitions. • continuing unsuccessful attempts at coordinating movements to the rhythm of the music.	Responds by: • using a variety of movements. • continuing unsuccessful attempts at coordinating movements to the rhythm of the music. • moving to music with a partner. Responds to fast and slow. New responses are influenced by home musical environment.
SINGING (Vocalizing, Chanting)			
Attempts to sing short songs. Begins to imitate words of a song.	Continues to imitate words of a song. Begins to: • sing spontaneously in everyday activities. • imitate rhythms and melodies of a song. • model singing	Continues to sing spontaneously. Sings alone, not in groups. Sings longer songs and sings them more often than when a baby. Learns a song by chanting words and	Begins to sing correct words, rhythm, and melody of a song. Likes to: • invent new songs • make new arrangements of familiar songs. • play singing games.

UNBORN	BIRTH TO THREE MONTHS	THREE TO SIX MONTHS	SIX TO NINE MONTHS	NINE TO TWELVE MONTHS

PLAYING INSTRUMENTS

LISTENING	MOVING
Becomes aware of and identifies: • steady beat • sound and silence • singing voice • difference in sounds (timbre) Identifies: • same/different • up/down/same • high/low • Long/short • Fast/slow Experiences: • a variety of moods in music • music accompanied by instruments or other voices • Hymn tunes	Experiences: • Moving to steady beat • Matching rhythm patterns by clapping, patchen, and on rhythm instruments. • Moving to a variety of tempos • Moving appropriately to different moods in music. • Clapping the rhythm of words of songs. • Starting and stopping with the music.

TWELVE TO EIGH-TEEN MONTHS	EIGHTEEN TO TWENTY-FOUR MO.	TWO YEARS	THREE YEARS
	after adults' singing	rhythm (age 2½). Range for song selection: C-A	• sing songs imitating animals or environmental sounds. Range for song selection: C-A

PLAYING INSTRUMENTS

			Explores a variety of: • environmental sounds. • homemade instruments. • classroom instruments.

FIVE YEARS

SINGING	PLAYING INSTRUMENTS
Finds the singing voice through: • Imitating a variety of sounds • Making up singing conversations • Singing alone and in small-and-large-group settings Experiences singing melodic patterns that: • are same/different • move up/down/same • are high/low • are fast/slow Experiences: • Singing games • Folk songs • Hymn fragments • Accompanied and unaccompanied songs • Ostinati • Songs of different moods Becomes aware of good posture Sings most songs in middle C to A range	Experiences: • Playing a variety of environmental, homemade, and classroom instruments. • Playing sounds that are: + Same/different + Move up/down/stay the same + Fast/slow + Express a variety of moods • Echoing rhythm patterns • Playing the rhythm of the words of songs • Playing songs with rests • Playing ostinati

FOUR AND FIVE YEARS

READING MUSIC	PERFORMING
Identifies through picture symbols: • Steady beat • Long/short sounds • High/low • Same/different pitches	Shares musical experiences with parents and others during choir.

GENERAL MUSIC UNDERSTANDINGS	CHURCH MUSIC UNDERSTANDINGS
Rhythm Musical sounds: • Have a steady beat • Can be long or short **Pitch and Melody** Musical sounds: • Can be same or different • Can move up or down • Can be high or low **Form** Musical sounds: • Can be grouped into same and different patterns • Can be organized into same and different phrases **Expressive Qualities** Music can: • Be fast or slow • Be loud or soft • Express moods or feelings **Harmony** Songs can be sung: • With or without accompaniment • With ostinati	**Music in Worship** • Music can be used to praise God • Music helps a person talk to God • Music helps people express their feelings to God • Music is an important part of church activities • Musical instruments help people praise God **Music in the Christian Life** • Music helps people learn about Jesus • Music helps families have a happy time • God gives people music to enjoy • Music makes working and playing with others enjoyable **Hymnology** • Music helps people learn about God's world • People write songs that others can sing to God • People can sing Bible verses and thoughts **Music in Outreach and Missions** • Music is a way to tell others about Jesus

Personal Learning Activities

1. Understanding Preschoolers
Name one way in which an unborn child responds to music. Choose one word which describes the four-year-old's way of thinking. Choose several words to describe the five-year-old's concept of sharing.

2. Meeting the Special Needs of Preschoolers
Identify ways that a leader of a preschool music group can help handicapped children, children from different ethnic backgrounds, and children from troubled home situations. Name two ways to help preschoolers deal with divorce, blended families, and death.

3. Laying Spiritual Foundations
Name the nine areas in which preschoolers develop spiritual understandings through musical experiences. Identify at least one concept in each area.

4. Laying Musical Foundations
Name five areas in which preschoolers develop musical understandings. Identify at least one concept in each area.

5. Laying Church Music Foundations
Name four areas in which preschoolers develop church music understandings. Identify at least one concept in each area.

6. Organizing for Preschoolers
Who gets first consideration when organizing musical experiences for preschoolers? What is the best ratio of leaders to preschoolers for four- and five-year-olds? What is the best ratio of leaders to preschoolers for three-year-olds? What is the most significant question to answer in determining when an organization should meet? After Christian commitment, list three other important leader qualifications.

7. Planning Musical Experiences for Preschoolers

What should be the choice of curriculum materials for Southern Baptist preschool music groups and choirs? Describe the contents of a typical issue of *The Music Leader*. Name at least two other curriculum materials produced by the Sunday School Board for preschool choir.

8. Enlisting Preschoolers

Identify those involved in sharing the responsibility for providing musical experiences for preschoolers. List three ideas for enlisting preschoolers.

9. Preparing Musical Activities for Babies, Ones, and Twos

List eight sources for potential leaders of preschool activities. How does the role of a leader in musical activities for babies through twos differ from that of a leader for fours and fives? What two types of songs are appropriate for use with babies, ones, and twos?

10. How Babies Through Twos Respond to Music

What is the unborn child's first response to music? What is the response experienced first by ones? What response is usually experienced first by twos?

11. Leading Musical Activities for Babies Through Twos

Name three types of musical activities for babies, ones, and twos. What is the purpose of offering music activity groups for younger preschoolers at church? What is the primary consideration in planning musical activities for babies, ones, and twos?

12. Preparing Musical Activities for Threes

Name two recommended approaches in developing a music activity group for threes. What room has the potential for being the best room arrangement for a music activity group? Name five learning centers that can be used in individual and small-group activities for threes. Describe an appropriate song for threes.

13. How Threes Respond to Music

Name four ways in which threes experience music. What do threes concentrate on first when learning a song? List three ways in which instruments can be used in a music activity group for threes.

14. Leading Musical Activities for Threes

Describe the ideal schedule for a music activity group for threes. What is the role of a leader in a music activity group for threes?

15. Preparing for Preschool Choir

What is the first and most significant step in becoming an effective preschool choir leader? What knowledge of preschoolers is necessary for planning appropriate activities for preschool choir? Of the five senses, name the three that play the lead roles in the music-learning process.

16. How Fours and Fives Respond to Music

List the four primary skills through which preschoolers develop concepts about music and describe an appropriate activity for each skill. What is the most significant activity in preschool choir?

17. Leading a Preschool Choir for Fours and Fives

Identify three significant decisions that must be made by a leader of fours and fives. Define *pacing*. List three nonmusical duties of a preschool choir leader.

The Church Study Course

The Church Study Course is a Southern Baptist education system designed to support the training efforts of local churches. It provides courses, recognition, record keeping, and regular reports for some 20,000 participating churches.

The Church Study Course is characterized by short courses ranging from 2 to 10 hours in length. They may be studied individually or in groups. With more than 600 courses in 24 subject areas, it offers 130 diploma plans in all areas of church leadership and Christian growth.

Complete details about the Church Study Course system, courses available, and diplomas offered may be found in a current copy of the *Church Study Course Catalog.*

The Church Study Course system is jointly sponsored by many agencies within the Southern Baptist Convention.

How to Request Credit for this Course

This book is the text for course number 10046 in the subject area: "Church Music Leadership." This course is designed for five hours of group study.

Credit for this course may be obtained in two ways:

1. Read the book and attend class sessions. (If you are absent from one or more sessions, complete the "Personal Learning Activities" for the material missed.)

2. Read the book and complete the "Personal Learning Activities." (Written work should be submitted to an appropriate church leader.)

A request for credit may be made on Form 725 "Church Study Course Enrollment/Credit Request" and sent to the Awards Office, Sunday School Board, 127 Ninth Avenue, North, Nashville, Tennessee 37234. The form on the following page may be used to request credit. Enrollment in a diploma plan may also be made on Form 725.

Within three months of your completion of a course, confirmation of your credit will be sent to your church. A copy of your complete transcript will be sent to your church annually during the July—September quarter if you have completed a course during the previous 12 months.